P9-DMO-103

Earl Campbell

THE DRIVING FORCE

Earl Campbell

THE DRIVING FORCE

Sam Blair

WORD BOOKS
PUBLISHER
WACO, TEXAS

Frontispiece: Thanksgiving 1979. Earl Campbell stiff-arms Dallas's Cliff Harris as he speeds toward his second touchdown of the day

(PHOTO: Eliot Kamenitz, Dallas *Morning News*).

EARL CAMPBELL: THE DRIVING FORCE

Copyright © 1980 by Sam Blair.
All rights reserved. No portion of this book
may be reproduced in any form, or transmitted in any form
or by any means, electronic or mechanical, including
photocopy, recording, or any information storage
and retrieval system, without written
permission from the publisher.

ISBN 0-8499-0259-2
Library of Congress Catalog Card number: 80-51486
Printed in the United States of America.

For Karen, Jason, and Collin—the First Team

CONTENTS

1. Different Roads 9
2. A Place to Grow 19
3. Moving Up 31
4. Taking Off 41
5. Choosing the Longhorns 53
6. Big Moments—and Misery 61
7. That Perfect Autumn 79
8. Hello, Heisman 93
9. Losing—and Winning 101
10. Striking Earl 109
11. A Boomer for Boomtown 119
12. That Special Spring 133
13. Giving Some More 143
14. Blasting Fast 157
15. The Greatest Rewards 169

DIFFERENT ROADS 1

Superstars, remember, perform by different standards. Their fair days are good and their good days are great. For Earl Campbell, Thanksgiving Day 1979 was a great one. . . . .

HANDS ON HIS KNEES, he stands slightly crouched 7 yards behind the line of scrimmage, listening to quarterback Dan Pastorini yell signals above the roar of the crowd in Texas Stadium. It's early in the first quarter, third down and one yard to go on the Houston 39, and it seems this will be a routine play. It isn't.

As the Oiler linemen settle into their stance, Earl Campbell is vaguely aware of the goal line 61 yards beyond them. But mainly he watches the Dallas defense. The Cowboys have pulled two linebackers and the left cornerback up so close that they are confronting him with a seven-man line.

Oiler center Carl Mauck snaps the football to Pastorini and the field is a blur of action. Campbell angles toward his right, takes the ball from Pastorini, and hesitates slightly as his blockers go to work. Tight end Mike Barber bangs linebacker D. D. Lewis inside, spinning him out of the play. Cornerback Benny Barnes charges 2 yards across the line, hoping to tangle the play before it gets untracked, but fullback Tim Wilson, who has lined up just in front of Campbell in the I formation, veers out and blocks him. Earl, running low and starting to accelerate, zips behind Wilson.

One yard past the line Campbell cuts sharply toward the right sideline while right guard Ed Fisher, pulling out of the line and swinging behind Barber's block, slams into middle linebacker Bob Breunig. Breunig keeps his feet but loses a step of pursuit he can't afford. He is 4 yards away from Campbell and a step behind free safety Cliff Harris, who is trying to cut Campbell off. It's a futile attempt.

Campbell finds the sideline at the Dallas 45, and points himself goalward with Harris a step behind. Breunig and cornerback Aaron Kyle try to get in the race. This is the Cowboys' stadium, but most of the capacity crowd of sixty-five thousand fans is cheering. They're watching the National Football League's premier runner—a Texas legend.

Suddenly Campbell's stride widens, his thick body leaning toward the goal line as he pulls away, the ball swinging rhythmically in his right hand. Harris and Breunig fall away at the 30, and Kyle dives desperately at the 25. Earl kicks his bulging legs a little higher and moves on, knowing he's home free at the 20. Two teammates, Barber and Rob Carpenter, race in his wake, their arms raised as he crosses the goal line. They rush up and embrace him, for this run has brought the Oilers nose and nose with their more celebrated upstate rivals in the NFL. Campbell waits calmly for an approaching official, then hands over the ball.

After Earl's spectacular run the score is even at 7–7, but the Cowboy offense also is playing furiously. Slightly more than two minutes before halftime, Dallas holds a 21–10 lead and the Oilers, facing first-and-ten on the Cowboy 27, are anxious for another touchdown.

The defense isn't drawn in quite so tightly this time,

and the Oilers are using a different formation. Campbell is the single back, lined up 5 yards deep with two tight ends on the line and wide receivers Guido Merkens and Mike Renfro on the wings. This time Campbell slashes off the left side of his line and finds room as left tackle Leon Gray blocks defensive end Harvey Martin inside and tight end Rich Caster takes linebacker Mike Hegman outside. Campbell bursts through the gap, and at the 21 he swerves toward the left side of the goal line.

Harris leaps for him at the 18, but Earl, veering away, thrusts his right hand on Harris's helmet in a perfect stiff-arm, and Harris falls helplessly to the turf. Campbell widens his stride, and suddenly he's gone. He lopes across the end zone and, while Renfro runs behind him holding one finger high, carefully puts the ball on the turf and circles back toward the Houston bench.

It was one of the proudest moments in the history of the Houston Oilers—a 30–24 win—Houston's first victory over the Cowboys in a regular-season game. As the players whooped, whistled, and soul-slapped their way up the ramp to the locker room, their down-home coach, Bum Phillips, waved his cream-colored cowboy hat triumphantly at the cheering crowd. His crewcut hair and wire-rimmed glasses glistened in the lights as he strode proudly off the field.

"The Cowboys may be America's Team," he said, "but we're Texas's team. I wouldn't have it any other way."

Phillips was well aware that much of the credit for the victory belonged to his five-foot, eleven-inch, 224-pound running back. Earl Campbell had carried thirty-three times for 195 yards, scored two touchdowns, and made the Dallas defense vulnerable to Pastorini's passing. It was the most spectacular performance of his second pro season, and it was exactly what Phillips had hoped for when he had made the deal which allowed Houston to draft Campbell No. 1 out of the University of Texas in 1978.

It was no surprise to Cowboy coach Tom Landry either. "Campbell was brilliant," he said. "We had to get up on the line of scrimmage to stop him, and when we did, they hit a couple of bombs. He is just an awesome runner."

Cowboy defensive end John Dutton was equally impressed. "We went into the game trying to first stop Campbell and then Pastorini," he said. "We didn't stop Campbell and we didn't put pressure on Pastorini. They had us guessing all day. Campbell is a great runner. All I did was try to grab him and hold on for dear life."

Brilliant. Awesome. Great.

Those adjectives flow naturally when people salute Earl Campbell. Fans in football-crazy Texas have watched him rush along the road to superstardom since his high school days in Tyler, a city one hundred miles east of Dallas which, until Campbell, was most famous for its roses. They have seen him become the driving force behind every team for which he has played, helping to lift each to tremendous success throughout his record-breaking career.

Yet there was a time when Earl was running a different road, and the odds weighed heavily against his ever making it big—or making it at all. He was "Bad Earl," a confused teenager caught up in drinking, smoking, and fighting, with no idea what he wanted out of life. But he did have a support system that would not let him go—his family, coaches, his girlfriend—people who believed in him and helped him see that there was more for him in life than honky tonks and pool halls. Earl listened, although it took a long struggle within himself. And today he believes he is what he is because of faith, family, and football.

Earl Campbell has a long jaw which gives his face a solemn, sometimes sullen appearance until he smiles. He speaks in a slow, soft voice and isn't the type to get heavy with anyone.

"I don't really say I don't like someone," he explained once. "I say I don't like what they do. They have a right to feel the same way about me.

"For instance, I dip Skoal. Lots of people smoke cigarettes, so I say, 'Hey, don't you blow your smoke in my face and I won't spit my Skoal in yours.'"

Kicking the cigarette habit as a schoolboy has proved

very rewarding for Earl. On Loop 323 near John Tyler High School stands a highway signboard bearing this message:

Skoal, Brother!
A Pinch Is All It Takes!

Beside the words is a huge autographed picture of Earl. It was reported that in 1979 he earned $350,000 from endorsements of various products, and the Skoal account is one of his largest.

Earl now makes more money in a year than he once dreamed could be had in a lifetime, but still he treasures most the people who are closest to him and those who have helped him win—his coaches; Reuna, the girl who has stuck by him since junior high; his teammates; his brothers and sisters. Most of all, his mother . . .

Ann Campbell exudes strength, warmth, and a genuine concern for people. She is a large woman with gray hair and a smile which spreads slowly across her face and then remains fixed when she has stopped talking. Earl has her smile, and a lasting respect for how she urged her children to work and achieve.

For Ann Campbell is the real driving force behind her son's success. "I understand that fellow Lombardi was a great motivator," Earl says, "but he couldn't teach my Mama anything."

Widowed when Earl was eleven, Ann Campbell struggled to raise ten children by herself in a small wooden house outside Tyler. Life was hard, and the family was poor, but Ann Campbell provided her children with a rich heritage of faith, integrity, love, and hard work. The Campbell family enjoyed a rare spiritual wealth which made life in that old house something special. Despite second-hand clothes and never having enough money, Earl and his brothers and sisters knew theirs was a good life. "We're poor," he said as a college senior, "but we're rich in a lot of ways."

Earl's friends can attest to that. High school teammate

Lynn King remembers, "There were holes in the floor and the kitchen floor kinda sunk from one end to the other. It was low rent all the way, but those people were great. There was no resentment, no racism. I tell you, Earl's mother is super."

"That old house wasn't fancy," seconds Ken Dabbs, the University of Texas recruiting coordinator who came to know the family well through his frequent visits with Earl, "but in that home was as much warmth and love as I've ever been around. They all knew they had a responsibility and they did it.

"You can walk in some homes and, if the friendship and love are not there, it doesn't take you long to find it out. But this home had it all."

Darrell Royal, who won the college recruiting battle for Earl and coached him through his junior year at Texas, also feels the Campbell family had something special.

"There are two big factors you'll find in that home," Royal notes. "One is pride, and the other is love. Those are two strong factors to start any relationship from, and they've got an abundance of both.

"They're as honest as they can be. They're full of integrity. And that has to come from the mother. She's a lady of great pride and a lot of confidence, and she has instilled a lot of that in Earl.

"I know the last year I coached and we had that 6–6 tie with Oklahoma, I felt terrible. I was dejected and bent over with my hands on my knees because I really was kinda sick, feeling woozy in my stomach. Somebody snapped a picture of me like that and it was in the paper. Well, she saw it and wrote me the nicest letter you've ever read, and really gave me a little bit of reaming out.

"She told me she didn't want to see me with my head down ever, that I ought to be proud. She finished it by saying, 'Always remember that there's a man higher who looks low.'

"That letter was written in pencil and I still have it in my scrapbook. I wouldn't take anything for it. You can see the way she is with her friends and folks she's close to, so you can imagine how she talked to those kids."

As Earl grew into a young man, his personality and his attitude toward people benefited from his mother's guidance. "He has the ability," former high school coach Corky Nelson says, "to relate to all kinds of people—rich, poor, black, white. It doesn't matter; he's just the same old Earl. And that's what I love about him."

Having known hardship as a child, Earl makes a special effort to help those who find themselves in difficulty. He returned to Tyler in February of 1980 to appear at a benefit program for Traci Kenner, a former majorette from his old junior high school who had been paralyzed in an automobile accident. In Houston he sponsored the Earl Campbell Crusade for Kids, appearing on television and asking people to donate old books, school supplies, and toys to underprivileged children. His appeal produced a truckload. Then he bought some notebooks and lunchboxes and handed out everything at the parks.

"Through his example and through his strength," says Fred Akers, the Texas head coach in Earl's final splendid season as a Longhorn, "I've become a better person for having known him."

Earl likes to share his success with those nearest him. He won the Seagram's Seven Crowns Athlete of the Year award after his rookie season, and received a $10,000 cash prize. "This is money I wasn't planning on," he told Don Smith, public relations director for the Seagram's program. "I'll just put it in savings and let my baby sister and brother use it for college."

Before he reported to training camp for his second Oiler season, he gave his fiancée Reuna a $34,000 Mercedes 450 SEL, but was embarrassed that it became public knowledge. "Making people happy," he said, "is what life is all about."

Campbell is quiet, slow to anger, a guy who'll try to avoid the spotlight rather than dominate it. To some extent this has hurt his press relations in Houston. Some regulars on the Oiler beat complain he's difficult to reach off the field, and when they do reach him he has little to say.

He's uncomfortable with mass interviews, although he comes across much better in a one-on-one situation.

This is due in part to a natural shyness; in part to a sensitivity about how all the media attention may look to his teammates. Earl is known for his team spirit and loyalty to his fellow players. In his rookie year, when a lot of people began referring to the team as the Houston Earlers, he objected. "I want them to be Houston Oiler fans," he said, "not Houston Earler fans." Commenting on his unselfish nature, David Casstevens wrote in *The Houston Post*, "If it were up to Earl, he probably would change the name of the I formation to the 'We.' "

His teammates appreciate his attitude. Dan Pastorini, the Houston quarterback for Campbell's first two seasons, says, "He's the best ball carrier I've ever seen, and the finest human being I've ever known."

Houston's offensive linemen will second that. Earl always has treasured the guys up front who block for him, and now he shows it with gifts. After his rookie season he gave each starting lineman a gold necklace. His second year, when they gathered for the first day of training camp at Angelo State University in San Angelo, Texas, Earl gave each of them a gold money clip shaped like a spur, inscribed with the lineman's name and "1,450 Yards—1978."

Bum Phillips knows that Campbell is an athlete with a special feeling for the team.

"We might have gotten another great runner with a different personality, and he might have come in and clashed with our players," the Oiler head coach says. "But from the day this kid got here he's acted like 'Man, I'm lucky to be here.'

"That's why I don't think he'll ever change. He's got everything a guy can get, and he still acts like he ain't got nothin'."

Earl's faith runs as deep as his talent. It is part of his heritage from his mother, and it is the other dynamic force in his life that drives him forward. At the same time, his faith keeps him on a steady keel.

"Every Sunday noon in training camp Earl comes in

the dining room in his suit and tie," Bum says. "He just came from church. That's something that's *in* him.

"He believes in what the Lord teaches, not in the parts he wants to believe. Earl's not one of those vote dry, drink wet Christians."

"I love going to church because, just like going to practice, you can learn something," Earl says. "I'm no saint. I fall short just like everyone else. The key is falling short and then trying to get back up, just like after a busted play.

"The Lord has been very instrumental in my life. When I'm with him I feel like I have that extra kick."

It's a long way from the rose fields of Tyler to the oil fields of Houston. Junior high school teammate David Wells points out, "If you see Earl now, and knew him then and what kind of problems and hardships he had to deal with, it's unbelievable. It all sounds too good to be true, but it is."

Earl Campbell has made it. But he keeps his balance in the midst of all the fame and acclamation.

"Pro football is not something I'd like to do all my life," he says. "But you can come in with a smile and you can leave with a smile. It's not the living end, though. . . . Every guy who lives on God's green earth who may be doing good is stupid if he thinks he can't do better.

"I think a man should always dream of doing more and more."

A PLACE TO GROW 2

TYLER IS A TOWN that makes you feel good. It boasts the basics of East Texas landscape—sandy soil and pine trees—plus those nationally famous rose fields. In the fall when football is booming, Tyler is blooming. There are roses everywhere, and the sweetgum trees are riotous with their turning colors.

With a population of more than seventy thousand, Tyler is an attractive, progressive city in many ways, blessed with an abundance of lovely homes and considerable wealth. It is the business and cultural leader of its region, drawing quite a bit of money from the nearby oil fields and a tidy sum from its roses. Tyler grows as many as twenty million rosebushes a year, more than half the number sold in the U.S., and the rose industry provides a couple of thousand people with their living.

The city of Tyler sincerely celebrates the heroics of Earl Campbell, the black kid who made it big. And few doubt that Earl's success on the football field has helped race relations in this town. When the first blacks, Earl among them, integrated the once all-white Tyler schools, the attitudes of many people weren't far removed from the Old South.

Some of those same feelings obviously remain today in Tyler, as they do throughout the nation and world. But people regardless of color or creed could cheer on the same side when Earl Campbell led John Tyler High School to the state Class AAAA championship as an all-America halfback in 1973. His tremendous performances in college and professional football have strengthened that legacy.

Tyler is fortunate to have him as one of its own, but Earl also is fortunate in the timing of his career.

Had he been an outstanding football player during the 1960s, as older brothers Willie and Herbert were, he might have hit a dead end when he received his high school diploma. He would have played at a segregated school, Emmett Scott, and might have been a superstar who remained unknown to the big-time college scouts. But by the time he played he was able to compete at a large, well-known high school at the top level of the prestigious University Interscholastic League, whose football programs draw the attention of more college recruiters than any in America. And Southwest Conference schools were accelerating their recruitment of black athletes after some members first brought in a few in the middle and late '60s.

Had he been an outstanding football player in Tyler during the 1950s, Earl really would have known how it felt to be ignored. After I graduated from journalism school in 1954, my first job was on a Tyler newspaper, writing and editing sports. One day, on the eve of a big prize fight, I sent a photoengraving of the champion to the composing room to be run with the advance story. A few minutes later, I noticed one of the old heads from the composing room talking to one of the veteran editors in the newsroom. They glanced at me and then the composing room worker walked over to my desk.

"You can't run this," he said, holding out the photoengraving of the boxer. At first I thought he didn't understand the situation, and I explained this was the most logical picture to use with the big story.

Then he told me *I* didn't understand the situation, and explained that the paper never ran a picture of a black person.

"But this guy is the world champion," I said.

"Yep," the man said, "but he's still a nigger."

From then until Earl Campbell and the John Tyler Lions roared to the state championship in 1973, attitudes improved remarkably. Today, Earl and the roses give Tyler a good name—and deservedly so.

But, like almost anywhere else in the country, the city is not without flaws and occasional scandals. In one massive drug bust, 121 persons were charged with selling narcotics, a case which touched some of the city's most prominent families. That happened in April of 1979, two months after the wife of the Tyler police chief had been acquitted of the charge of murdering him in their home. The woman testified she shot him with a .38-caliber pistol after a terrifying experience at the family dinner table. She said he had been drinking heavily and had flown into a rage when their six-year-old daughter mentioned that she might one day marry a black. She said he threatened to kill her and their two daughters, and that she shot him when he returned to the house with a cased Thompson submachine gun.

That happened in Tyler, a city of pride and problems.

While talking about his childhood, Earl Campbell once said, "I tell people if they know where dirt is they know where this guy Earl came from. I started life with nothing but a lot of love and respect."

That and the name of the doctor who delivered him at home on March 29, 1955.

Almost twenty-five years later, when Earl was tearing through his second straight all-pro season with Houston, Dr. Earl Christian Kinzie sat in his office in the small town of Lindale and recalled Earl's birth. It was easy because

Dr. Kinzie, now seventy-two, had kept the details fresh, finding that a lot of people were curious about them since Earl started winning trophies and titles. His distinction, he found, made him a popular figure at everything from church socials to ocean cruises.

Lindale, which is seven miles from the Campbell home, also is quite proud of Earl. In a small confectionary and cafe just off Main Street an autographed picture is prominently displayed by the door. It's an eleven-by-fourteen action shot of Earl in the Texas-Oklahoma game, running over a Sooner player. And in the waiting room of Dr. Kinzie's clinic, a brick cottage shaded by a huge tree, is his own Earl Campbell gallery.

"Gee," he said, "I've enjoyed the reflected glory."

Dr. Kinzie, an osteopath, is white but had no restrictions about black patients when he saw Ann Campbell and many others thirty or more years earlier.

"I came from Kansas and was brought up in the Church of the Brethren," he said. "We preached the brotherhood of man and the fatherhood of God. We were taught God is color-blind."

Still, there were separate waiting rooms for blacks and whites.

"It was a crazy thing then," he said. "We examined them on the same examining table and they sat in the same chairs in our office. We used the same equipment. But socially they were separated. Colored people came in the side entrance and sat in a small room. Even today, some colored people feel more comfortable sitting there. I say, go where you are comfortable."

Dr. Kinzie delivered seven of the eleven Campbell children after Ann's brother recommended him to her. It was more convenient going to a doctor's office in Lindale instead of Tyler, and besides, Dr. Kinzie made house calls. He had come out to deliver Herbert and Alfred Ray before Earl and then the twins, Tim and Steve, after him. Later Ann went to his clinic for the birth of Martha and Margaret.

Ann had Earl by natural childbirth, and she and Dr.

Kinzie agreed it was a normal delivery, although their memories of the time of birth differ. Dr. Kinzie recalls coming to their house in darkness, either late at night or early morning. Ann says Earl was born between four and five o'clock in the afternoon and that her sister, Eva, was with her at the time.

"When he was born I really didn't have a name picked out," she recalls. "I said to my sister, 'What are we going to name him?' Dr. Kinzie said, 'Well, I'll just name this one after myself—Earl Christian.'"

Ann liked that.

"I'd always just known him as Dr. Kinzie. I didn't know he had that middle name, Christian. 'Earl Christian,' I said. 'That sounds fine to me.'"

Dr. Kinzie, delighted, held some old spring scales from the top by a diaper and weighed the baby. Then he wrote on the birth certificate:

"Earl Christian Campbell, eight pounds, two ounces."

On July 4, 1956, Dr. Kinzie returned and delivered twin boys. "Ann asked me to name them," he said, "so I gave them good ol' Bible names—Timothy and Stephen." A few years later, when the last of the girls arrived, Ann decided to name her Margaret in honor of Dr. Kinzie's first wife, who had died some years ago. So there are numerous ties between the old doctor in Lindale and the Campbell family. He treasures them.

On a cruise of Scandinavian countries in the summer of 1979, there was a get-acquainted social. Each passenger was asked to stand, introduce himself, and tell the others some personal background.

"I'm Dr. Earl Kinzie," he said. "I think it's only fair to tell you I did not write the Kinsey Report, but some of you people will be glad to know I did deliver the great Earl Campbell, who has my name."

That registered.

"From then on, I was a celebrity. Tom Law, a University of Texas regent from Fort Worth, said, 'I want to shake the hand that spanked Earl Campbell.'"

In 1979, when he at last had the money which would enable him to turn a long-standing dream into reality, Earl Campbell never considered asking his mother if she wanted her new house in the city. "I wouldn't want her out of the country," he said, "where she couldn't smell the morning air."

So he built her a house in Jones Valley, on land Earl's father had left the family. Jones Valley is a dozen miles from the heart of downtown Tyler—not terribly remote, but far enough to be open and relaxed, just as Ann Campbell remembered from the time she was a small girl. The new home fronts on Farm Road 492, and just fifty feet down a sandy slope sits the old Campbell homestead, a faded old wooden house on Texas College Road, a blacktop which winds through the trees and farm land toward Tyler. Just across the intersection of the two roads there's a junkyard. Some might consider it an eyesore, particularly located so near that lovely antique brick home with its circular drive and landscaped lawn. But Ann Campbell pays it no mind. Jones Valley is dear to her, and it's where she always wants to be.

"I love the country—not being jammed right underneath people," she said when she still lived in the old house. "My husband wanted us to move to town after we had our second child, but I didn't go for it. The country is my home."

After moving into her new house, she reflected on how her roots were so firmly planted in this certain part of Smith County, Texas.

"I've been right here on this corner for thirty-two years," she said. "I *love* it! I really do." The room filled with her warm laughter. Clearly there is no place else on earth Ann Campbell would rather live.

Her parents, Reuben and Lizzie Collins, moved her and nine other children to a farm two-and-a-half miles from her present home when she was six years old. They were tenant farmers, although her father, a strict, hard-working, religious man, dreamed of the day he might own that land.

"I tell you I picked many a boll of cotton on that land,"

Ann Campbell says. "And it had an orchard. We used to grow peaches, chop cotton, pull corn and peanuts. My daddy was a big farmer. But everything you raised then was so cheap. Somehow or other he just never could get on his feet. He worked so hard and bargained for that land, but he lost it."

That was during the Great Depression of the 1930s, when millions of Americans were struggling to survive. Reuben Collins's daughter Ann never dreamed then that she would someday have a son who would make enough money from football to buy the place, when her daddy couldn't make enough from farming it.

After Earl joined the Oilers, a real estate agent called Ann and told her it was for sale. "Mrs. Campbell, I'm not trying to help Earl spend his money," he said, "but this land surely would be a nice investment for him."

She thanked him for calling, although she made no promises.

"Earl knew all about that land," she says. "He'd heard me talk about growing up on that farm, and he had once had a summer job there hauling hay. Well, Earl called later that day and I told him about it. He got pretty excited.

"He said, 'You mean that property Papa Rube once bargained for? Oooh, nothing would please me better than to get my Roots Land back!' "

So the deal was made and Ann Campbell, so happy with her home in Jones Valley, found added comfort from knowing the old farm now was in the family.

"When I got married," she recalls fondly, "I married from that property."

As a teen-ager she rode a bus into Tyler to attend Emmett Scott High School, an all-black school in a totally segregated district. Shortly after she graduated in June, 1942, Ann Collins married B. C. Campbell, a young man from a neighboring farm in Jones Valley.

He soon was called into service for World War II and sent overseas, so Ann lived in town with relatives until he came home. In 1946 she gave birth to a son, Willie, the first of their eleven children. A little later B. C. inherited fourteen acres of family property. He built a house, and they moved in when Willie was one year old.

Earl was the sixth child. Before he was born in 1955 there were two other boys, Herbert and Alfred Ray, and two girls, Evelyn and Ruby. Earl was followed by the twins, Tim and Steve, then two more girls, Martha and Margaret, and finally another boy, Ronnie.

All through those years and since, as Ann did when she was a small girl, they attended Hopewell Baptist Church No. 1.

This one is not the Hopewell Baptist Church you find about a mile up Farm Road 492 from her house. Hopewell No. 1 is several miles more distant, on the Van Highway, another country church filled with old-time religion and values.

"People tease me about passing the church near me to go to my church, but it's very important to me," she said. "I went to that church in a wagon with my parents and I joined there as a child. I'll always remain there.

"That day I went down the aisle and gave the preacher my hand I didn't know the Lord like I know him now. Then, your parents carried you there and you just joined the church. It was the tradition. When I was grown and married I really got to know the Lord. This didn't come about through one special experience. I just felt close to him in my life."

B. C. Campbell is remembered as a fine man who worked hard for his family. He had grown up raising roses as well as other crops on the farm, and as his own family grew he relied strongly on his expert ability as a budder to help make a living.

Dick Atwood, whose father owned a nursery, often saw B. C. display his skill, taking a limb from a bush and tying it into a seedling, which a year later would produce roses.

"B. C. budded for a lot of nurseries, including my daddy's, and he worked on a contract basis," Atwood said. "The pay back in the '50s was $2.50 per thousand, and a good budder could do two-and-a-half to three thousand in a day. Jobs were hard to find then, and a good budder could make more contracting than working by the hour."

When his children were quite young, B. C. Campbell began teaching them how to raise roses.

"When I was five, he took me to the fields," Earl said. "He took all of us older kids, and that was very important to us later. Before he passed on, he taught us how to work in the rose fields."

Ann Campbell and her children proved they learned their lessons well. Earl and some of the other children, who became expert budders just as their father, hired out to nurseries around Tyler. And Ann for years helped support her family by working in the rose fields behind their house, a practice she continued until she moved into her new home. (Roses, as you might imagine, made a lasting impression on the Campbell family. In college Earl had a plaque on his bureau: "Some people look at a rose bush and see the thorns; others look at a thorn bush and see the roses.")

In 1965, the house where Earl and four of his brothers had been born burned, and in December their father bought a house from a family which also had eleven children and moved it to his land. It was the frame house which still stands today. It had three bedrooms and only about nine hundred square feet of floor space, but it seemed adequate at a time when so many of the children were small. (They slept three to a bed, Earl sharing one with Herbert and Alfred.)

The house needed painting and some repairs, and B. C., who was keeping busy with his regular work although he hadn't felt well, hoped to take care of it soon.

But one afternoon in the spring of 1966, B. C. came in from the rose fields and told his wife, "I'm just sick." He had seen Dr. Kinzie several times for a liver condition, and Dr. Kinzie, after examining him again, referred him to a hospital in Tyler for treatment.

Nine days later he suffered a heart attack and died, just hours before he was to be transferred to the Veterans' Hospital in Shreveport, Louisiana. It was May, a beautiful time of year in the East Texas countryside, a time when some of the children would have been out working with their father. But suddenly he was gone.

There were ten children still at home, ranging from high school age to three years old. Willie, who had entered military service after graduating from Emmett Scott High School, would receive a discharge and return home to help any way he could, but Ann Campbell knew she faced a tremendous responsibility now. Some of her children also sensed it immediately.

"I'll never forget the day I came home from the hospital after my husband died," she says. "The children had already heard the news. Earl was sitting by himself on the front porch. He looked up at me and said, 'Mama, now that this has happened, let's have the funeral and get it over with.' "

Earl was eleven then, and grieving for his father as much as anyone, but he sensed the urgency of putting the family's life in motion again. And his mother, fully aware of her burden, was determined that she and her children would stay together and grow together—working, learning, respecting others and believing in God.

"I set 'em down and talked to 'em," she remembers. "I told them I was by myself now, and I had to have their help. I told them I would put clothes on their backs and food in their mouths but that I couldn't afford to pay their fines if they got in jail. If they got in trouble with the police, they'd just have to take care of it themselves."

Ann Campbell had always told her children, "A tub has to sit on its own bottom." Those words took on even greater meaning now. The older ones realized they must contribute any way they could, and the younger ones would also learn about responsibility as they grew.

Ann worked cleaning other people's homes, as she had done before her husband died, and she stayed busy in the rose fields with her kids. Somehow, they always made it. What little money they had for clothes they spent at the Salvation Army store, and the children never refused to wear other people's hand-me-downs. Earl got free lunch at school by washing dishes. At home they grew most of the food they needed; in the spring Ann would slaughter a calf or a hog so the family could have beef or pork for the year.

And every Sunday they went to Hopewell Baptist No. 1 and thanked God for what they had. Most of all, of course, they had each other.

When her husband died, Ann Campbell recalled once, she "saw the opportunity to jump out and do a lot of other things, but I was determined to stay here and raise these children. When my husband died I had a job cleaning house twelve miles from home, over on the other side of the junior college. I quit that job and took one for less pay to be nearer home and closer to my children.

"There never was a time when I really thought I wouldn't make it alone," she said. "You can do it if you have enough love and determination. It's all in the individual, and in what you want to do with your life.

"I knew there was going to be a lot of work for all of us. But I never had any lazy kids. They always knew how to work—their father taught them that before he died. We knew we'd all have to work and share in this together."

Those years are etched deeply in Earl's memory. He has never ceased to marvel at how strong and loving his mother remained in a situation where others soon might have crumbled.

"The way Mama raised all of us is unbelievable," he said. "She always told us, 'We can make it. We may not have everything, but we can make it.'"

The Rev. John Westbrook, a former Baylor running back who came to know the Campbells while pastoring Tyler's True Vine Baptist Church, now is Earl's minister at Houston's Antioch Baptist. He looks at Ann Campbell today, when the family can live comfortably in the aura of Earl's football success, and he's equally impressed.

"Earl's mama always has been a very strong woman of keen insight," Westbrook says. "All this glamor has not made her lose sight of the fact that she's the mother of several children. Her head hasn't swollen. She still knows who she is, where she's from, where she's going. She would tell you all of this stuff is temporary, but God is real.

"She still works. That's integrity. Some people in her position would say, 'I have a son who will take care of me the rest of my life. I'll take it easy.' But she sticks with the basic beliefs which have guided her life and her children. Her attitude is, 'All this stuff could be taken away tomorrow, but if we have each other we can survive.' "

Because of her deep and abiding faith, Ann Campbell faced the future with confidence when her husband died. Years later she still lives happily and proudly in Jones Valley on that corner "right where my husband left me." Others may feel she faced overwhelming odds, but she always felt she had the best possible help. "We're all the same in God's eyes," she says.

When times got extra tough she would always remember the words of a friend at Hopewell Baptist No. 1: "The harder the cross, the brighter the crown."

MOVING UP 3

On March 8, 1980, Earl arose at 5:30 A.M. and drove seventy-five miles north from his Houston home to Huntsville, headquarters of the Texas Department of Corrections. There he spent the day with the Bill Glass Prison Crusade, talking and visiting with inmates in four different units.

Glass, once an all-American lineman at Baylor University and a star defensive end for the Cleveland Browns in the 1960s, is an evangelist who visits prisons throughout the nation. He takes famous athletes with him, because they communicate and relate well with the inmates. In Campbell he noticed a sensitive, intimate feeling for those in the audience, particularly the young men at the Ferguson unit, where almost all inmates are eighteen to twenty-one years of age.

Campbell, wearing boots, slacks, sports jacket, open-collar shirt, and a gold necklace, stood on the stage, smiling and giving a soft-sell testimony. The inmates, with their close-cropped hair and plain white uniforms, listened in-

31

tently. "How many of you guys from Tyler?" Campbell asked.

Maybe ten men raised their hands. He asked each to stand and talked to him individually. Then he told the entire audience, "I was like some of you guys until I went to high school. But then I committed my life to Christ."

He was talking about his "Bad Earl" period, a time of his life which didn't pass quickly or without a tormenting struggle with himself. But because he came out of it, all the happiness and success since have been that much sweeter.

"In order to appreciate the good things," Earl has often said, "you got to be down."

He was certainly down then, a kid who smoked his first pack of Kool cigarettes when he was in the sixth grade and who, by the time he was in junior high school, was carousing and drinking, running with older guys, and shooting pool. He never got into drugs, but he was hanging out in dives where ultimately he might wind up in jail. (One place, the Eight Ball was better known among its patrons as The Cut because that's what happened to a lot of them there.) And Ann Campbell had made it clear that any child of hers who managed to get himself into jail would also have to manage to get himself out.

Ann Campbell believed there was something much better inside her son than he realized then. "Earl was going over Fool's Hill," she says. "He was smoking two packs of cigarettes a day, drinking a few beers, doing a little gambling. He was hanging out with the wrong crowd of guys and got kinda wild. I finally sat him down and gave him a talking to. I told him to get hold of himself. If he did, he could go places in life."

Earl listened, although he didn't change.

The Campbells' house in the country was seven miles from Loop 323, where Earl's buddies would often drop him off at night. He would run the rest of the way home, pulling his belt out of his jeans to beat off the dogs that chased him. All the while, he'd think of how his mother expected him to come closer to God and live for more than another big night in a honky tonk. He was touched and he was torn, but it was tough to stop his way of life.

So he kept running.

That's how he was, loving his mother and wanting to please her but also enjoying the rowdy life of Bad Earl, when he entered the ninth grade. It was 1970, and the Tyler Independent School District, to achieve racial integration, started busing students to different schools. Earl was transferred across town from Dogan Junior High to Moore Junior High, a previously all-white school. Ann Campbell, busy working in the rose fields behind their house and cleaning other people's homes to support her family, soon would receive some valuable help with her wayward son.

The head football coach at Moore, Lawrence LaCroix, also was black, and also new to the school. A native of New Orleans, LaCroix was a handsome, athletic man with a personality that quickly won the youngsters of both races. That fall LaCroix and assistant coach Al Harris, a white man, directed the ninth grade team which, led by halfback-linebacker Earl Campbell, won the city championship. But throughout that season he was doing a more important coaching job with Earl Campbell the person.

"Coach LaCroix always would sit me down and tell me about things outside of football," Earl recalls. "I guess it was like a father seeing potential in his kid when the kid can't see it himself. Lots of afternoons he'd give me a ride part of the way home, and he'd talk about how there could be so many good things ahead. 'Now, Earl, you can do it,' he'd say, 'but you've got to do it this way because this is right.' "

Then LaCroix would drop Earl off at Texas College Road, leaving him with his thoughts on that long run home.

About the same time, the one great romance of Earl's life was building. Reuna Smith, a bright, lovely girl, lifted his heart each time he saw her at school. They began dating, and as they grew closer she too became a valuable influence. She was more outgoing than Earl, a sweet girl and a good student and citizen. In her way Reuna encouraged him as much as LaCroix did.

"I had so many times when I felt weak or downhearted but Reuna never let me quit," Earl says. "She always loved me and encouraged me. 'Earl, you can do it,' she'd tell me. 'Tomorrow will be better.'"

Earl knew he had some wonderful people pulling for him and this weighed on him. "I always felt a responsibility," he says, "because others expected more of me. My mother, my girlfriend, my coach, they all felt I had more to give."

But he kept holding back, clutching his old ways and all the while wondering what he needed to make him let go. Then he found the way. One night he was running that road and slowed to rest.

"I remember it like yesterday," Earl says. "I was walking down by an old pine tree and felt kinda lost. I just looked up and said, 'Lord, I need your help. Please, Lord, give me the strength to help myself.'"

The help came. Earl began to feel the strength and guidance of a driving force.

"All that stuff I had done before was over," he says, "I just completely stopped it one day. No more drinking, no more smoking, no more running around. I started working hard and pushing myself."

Bad Earl was gone, but he'll never be forgotten. Campbell believes those years were important to his life. "I'm proud of everything that happened to me before," he says. "It made me the man I am today."

"Hey, Earl," said one of the kids from Tyler he met that day at the state prison, "are you still kinda down-home, or have you let all this go to your head?"

"I think I'm still down-home," Earl replied. "The last time I was home my mama and I went and sat on the porch of our old house and talked about where I came from."

And when he is there he's out on that black-top road

every day, running to keep those powerful legs in shape. But instead of being chased by dogs, he now is followed by fans. If Earl runs, so do they. So it goes with a superstar down home.

The early days of integration in the Tyler schools were tense, uneasy, and sometimes a little scary. The mixing of the races went more smoothly at Moore Junior High, however, after the best white football player and the best black one mixed it with their fists one day.

David Wells and Earl Campbell remember their fight well.

"I walked in the restroom," Wells says, "and there was Earl. We both sort of muttered something to each other. We both were studs in school. He had been a stud in his old school and I felt like he was moving in on my territory. We just stared each other down and then we started fighting. We exchanged a few blows, and then the principal, Jim Trotter, caught us and hauled us into his office."

"David was about the same size as me," Campbell recalls, "and we fought to a draw, I guess. We became good friends afterward."

As boxers, they must have been pretty well matched. Earl weighed 180 pounds and probably was a little heavier, but David was a little taller. Their principal wasn't the least impressed.

"Mr. Trotter paddled us and then told us he didn't want us fighting, that we should set an example as students and athletes," Wells said. "Earl and I stood there looking and smiling at each other. Once we got the paddling we thought we'd proved ourselves to each other. We weren't scared of each other. We just wanted to be friends. After that we helped each other."

In that first year of integration at previously all-white Moore only 15 percent of the students were blacks; this made them especially apprehensive in their new surroundings. Earl and his twin brothers, Tim and Steve, who were entering the eighth grade, took one of the longest bus rides; they came from their farm northwest of Tyler, and Earl estimates they rode twenty-five miles to reach their new school on the far eastern edge of town. Other black students, like Earl's new sweetheart Reuna Smith, lived closer, but they also felt displaced.

"Those kids had been in another school the year before and expected to be there again," Jim Trotter says. "Then they were told they'd have to get on a bus and go to Moore—a white school in their way of thinking and a long way from home. It was a very traumatic experience. They didn't feel welcome.

"Earl did a lot for me that year. He was kind of the leader among black students, a calming force. We'd confer in my office, with David Wells representing the whites, and then they'd go out and help. I'll always have a soft spot in my heart for Earl Campbell, even if he'd never won the Heisman Trophy. He had a lot of friends of both races pretty soon. The students respected him."

Away from school Earl still had his problems. He was struggling through his Bad Earl period when he came to Moore, and although Trotter didn't know of his night life he sensed Earl was concerned about not pleasing his mother as he should.

"Sometimes he talked about his mama," Trotter says, "and how she wanted him to be a good Christian boy and to get along."

As long as he fell short, Earl knew she would send some withering looks in his direction.

"She's a great lady," he said years later, "but she's a terrible person to be on the bad side of. I'm her son and it took me a *long* time to get on her good side."

At that point, Earl's mother and family saw more ahead for him than he did.

"I didn't spend one minute thinking about the future," he says. "I thought one day I'd get out of school, get me a car and bum around."

But he did have one goal—to play football. He would work beside his mother, brothers, and sisters in the fields, raising roses, peas, potatoes, corn, and watermelons, but he was always wishing he could be on a football field.

"I *dis*encouraged Earl," Ann Campbell recalls, "but he always loved football. We'd go out in the field and work and when we'd come home Earl would be out in the yard throwing the football around. Or he'd be getting ready to run. I'd say, 'Earl, I thought you said you were tired.'"

In time she appreciated his love for football, however, for it brought him in close contact with coaches such as Lawrence LaCroix, who gave him important guidance and counseling in the years ahead.

LaCroix and his assistant coach, Al Harris, were concerned about developing a close-knit team in that first fall of integration. They felt that achieving harmony and a winning spirit on the football team would have a valuable effect on the entire student body.

"Lawrence and I talked about how we could bring the black and white kids together," Harris remembers, "and Earl helped us do it. He was quiet and shy, but he was a leader."

And LaCroix inspired Earl to do more, both when he spoke to him on the field and in the car after practice.

"Coach LaCroix was a dream to Earl," David Wells says. "He knew what kind of guy Earl was and he pushed him. He had a lot to do with Earl's success. But then he was good for all of us. He was a unique man and everybody loved him.

"When we first heard at Moore that we were getting a black coach we expected a bad time. We thought there would be a favoritism but there wasn't. If you deserved to play a position he'd stick you in there.

"Coach LaCroix had some kind of electricity or enthusiasm which excited everybody. A coach like him at that time was God's blessing. Some other coach might have messed Earl around, said, 'Hey, boy, get outta here.' He might have messed up a lot of us."

"Lawrence was a father figure to Earl and there was a mutual respect," Al Harris says. "He was a good coach who got along well with everyone, but he was particularly good communicating with Earl."

"He had great aspirations for Earl," Trotter noted. "Even then he talked about the Heisman Trophy. 'Earl,' he would say, 'you've got a chance.' "

In time all of this encouragement would pay off, but Earl was still behaving erratically, a fifteen-year-old kid confused about his priorities in life.

"Earl was wilder then," David Wells recalls. "He really didn't know what his future held for him. He carried a pack of cigarettes and smoked and really didn't have his head into football as much as he should have.

"He couldn't remember some of the plays. He'd say, 'David, what do I do on this play?' I'd say, 'You go straight up the guard's tail' or 'Around end.' "

Maybe this was just a part of growing up. For there was no question about Earl's desire to play football—or his ability. He already was a tremendous physical specimen. He weighed 180, and those years of hard work in the fields and running had helped him develop unusual strength in his upper body and legs.

"Earl always has been built like a weight lifter," David Wells says. "I saw that when he was only fourteen and I played basketball against him when he was still at Dogan. He fouled one of our smaller players and then I fouled him. We got in a scrap and knocked each other over some bleachers. He was strong, all right."

"At Moore Earl had strength," Lawrence LaCroix said years later. "But the thing that sticks out in my mind is his attitude. Earl was coachable. He wanted to learn."

For the blacks who rode a bus across town each morning it was tough to stay after school for practice. Earl and his twin brothers, who played on the eighth grade team, probably had as far to go home as anybody, but they always practiced.

"A kid that far away has to be dedicated to athletics to stay," Harris said. "We'd work out until five-thirty or six, and some evenings it was dark and cold and raining, but they stayed. We got some unity because of it, and I think those kids are a lot better off today because they stayed with it."

To Earl, the long journey home after practice wasn't nearly as much bother as having to lay out awhile with a broken bone in his wrist. A rule prohibited anyone playing in a game while wearing a cast, and after missing one game he felt he had to play in the next.

"On the day of the game Earl was absent from his fifth period class," Trotter recalls. "Later I saw him at the gym. I asked him, 'Earl, where's your cast?'

" 'The doctor took it off,' he told me. 'When?' 'Aw, a little while ago.' I told him, 'Wait a minute, Earl. I'm going to check this out.'

"The doctor hit the ceiling when I called. He said he hadn't removed the cast and that Earl needed to wear it another week. I told Earl he'd have to go back for a new cast and asked what had happened to the first one. He said, 'I went in the metal shop, got some steel cutters, and cut it off.' "

Wells remembers how determined Earl was when he attacked that cast. "He was mad and had the wild idea he was going to play. When he cut that cast off I grabbed it, had him autograph it, and took it home. I wanted to save it. I told myself, 'This ol' boy is gonna amount to something.' "

On the afternoon of the next game, the doctor was ready to remove the new cast. Trotter asked one of the school counselors to take Earl to the doctor's office, a two-mile drive. The counselor dropped Earl off and went to take care of some business, planning to return in thirty minutes.

Shortly after that, Trotter saw Earl back at school without the counselor.

"I asked him how he got back and he said, 'Aw, I just ran.' He was so anxious when the doctor told him he could play he was afraid he was going to miss the game if he waited on his ride."

Earl may have had some problems to work out in those days, but a lack of competitive spirit wasn't one of them.

That ninth grade year was a crucial year for Earl Campbell, the year he left Bad Earl behind and set his sights on better things. Lawrence LaCroix was an important figure in bringing about that change.

Years later, on March 2, 1979, John Tyler High School dedicated a new gymnasium and honored Earl Campbell for being the man he is by retiring his old jersey number— 20. Lawrence LaCroix was one of the featured speakers.

"We had our ups and downs," he said fondly, "but it seems now that all the downs have become ups."

That was one of the last times Earl would see his old coach. In August, while Earl was in training camp with the Oilers, LaCroix collapsed and died from a heart attack. But the words he spoke that day live on.

Indeed, all the downs have become ups.

TAKING OFF

THE SUMMER SUN BURNED DOWN, softening the tar on the road in front of the old house. In the rose fields out back, Earl Campbell felt like he had spent the day in a sauna.

It was like a lot of other days around the Campbell place that time of year. The work had to be done, no matter how much he sweated and hoped for even a little breeze. Then Earl saw that familiar green Volkswagen pulling in at his house and he smiled, pleased that he could go into the shade and visit with his coach awhile.

Earl didn't realize it, but this sweltering day was about to become very special for him.

It was 1973. In a few weeks he would report for his senior football season at John Tyler High School. For two years he had been one of the Lions' defensive stars at middle linebacker, and his great dream was to play the position in professional football. His first boyhood idol had been Dick Butkus, the Chicago Bears' bruising middle linebacker.

Earl had played some offense as a running back in the last few games of his junior season and he had been impressive, averaging 9.6 yards per carry, but that was secondary to him. He thrived on the life of a linebacker, crashing into ball carriers and pass receivers with a punishing force his opponents didn't forget.

Now Corky Nelson was telling him he must put this aside, that he would specialize as a running back his senior season. Earl was disappointed, and hurt.

"He told me I had to be the running back because we didn't have anybody else," he recalls, "and I started crying. I said, 'Well, I guess that ends my pro chance.'"

Of course, exactly the opposite proved to be true. But as they sat on the porch and talked that day, Nelson knew he had to sell his star on the change. Earl had gained weight each year, and was carrying 214 pounds while keeping his speed. His height still was five feet, eleven inches, however, and it appeared he would grow no taller.

"Earl really liked defense," Nelson said, "and I don't think he was sold on the fact that he was a running back, certainly not that he could be a great one. But I knew he had a dream of playing professional football and some day building his mother a house, and I tried to take the logical approach for him.

"I told him that he would be of marginal size for a pro linebacker, because it didn't look like he was going to be any taller. And I told him he had the size to be an outstanding pro running back. Then I said we felt we should turn him loose on offense that fall and just play him sparingly at linebacker. He was very apprehensive about the change, but he understood why I needed to do it then and that it was good for his future.

"He was still bothered by the idea when I left, but he was committed to giving his best shot as a running back."

As Nelson headed his car back toward Tyler he didn't know how much difference this would make that season. He did believe his inexperienced team might win a few more games with Earl running from their Veer and I formation offense.

"What Earl didn't realize, and what I didn't tell him was that we were going to build our entire offense around him," Nelson said. "We only had about four lettermen returning and three starters—our quarterback, our fullback and Earl. We didn't figure to win much so we just decided to let Earl carry the ball thirty times a game and see what happened."

What happened was John Tyler High School's best season in history. The Lions won fifteen games and lost none while sweeping to the Class AAAA championship of Texas. Earl made all-state, all-Southern, and all-American while rushing for 2,036 yards on 309 carries, a 6.6-yard average, and scoring twenty-eight touchdowns. He also completed three of four passes for 133 yards and one touchdown, played on all the punting, kicking, and return teams, and still played defense occasionally. In three games he started at linebacker and was the leading tackler in each.

"It was a great year," Earl remembers, "but I had a lot to learn as a runner. I guess I spent half that season punishing tacklers because I didn't know too much."

Yet the college scouts saw in this explosive and rugged runner with his massive legs and surprising speed a player with an unlimited future. Every school wanted to recruit him, and Earl was assured the opportunity for a college education. Beyond that his dream of professional football was alive and well.

In three years of high school he had come a long way. So had John Tyler High School.

From a distance the John Tyler campus, with its pine trees and cream-colored main building trimmed in blue, always looks peaceful. But in 1970–71, the first school year of integration, there was unrest in the student body. In the spring there was a walkout by a large number of blacks who felt they weren't treated fairly in some of the student elections, particularly the one for cheerleaders. The turmoil also touched the football program, and when the head coach's job was vacated at the end of the school year it seemed logical to seek a new man attuned to the times.

J. C. Prejean, athletic director for the Tyler schools, hired Corky Nelson, a coach in his early thirties with a solid background in integrated programs. Nelson had just served two years as an assistant coach at North Texas State University, which in 1956 had become the first senior college in the state to integrate its football team. Prior to that, Nelson had coached integrated teams in the San Antonio school system.

Nelson took over the program at Tyler without benefit of spring practice, so when the players reported for workouts in late August before the opening of school it was a time for getting acquainted and starting over. Nelson had to wait a little longer to get acquainted with Earl Campbell, however.

Although he had put his Bad Earl period behind him, Campbell still had a problem of basic immaturity, which isn't too unusual in a sixteen-year-old who has been cheered as a football hero.

"Earl had been allowed to do what he wanted to do and what he could do naturally in junior high," Nelson said. "I don't necessarily mean in athletics, but in school as a whole. Like most kids that age he took advantage of the situations. He was kind of spoiled when he got to high school.

"His sophomore year he reported a little late after we already had held some of our two-a-day workouts. Some people from the private Catholic high school had been talking with him about coming there, and I think he just wanted a little attention. So we told him he could come out, but that we would start him on our B team and he probably would play there for the whole year."

Nelson, who is white, was a firm disciplinarian and teacher, but he also was interested in his players personally. He helped Earl's situation when he added Lawrence La-Croix, who had worked so successfully with Earl at Moore Junior High, to his staff as backfield coach. LaCroix continued to be an important figure in the life of the young man whose own father had died when he was 11. But Earl would continue to struggle with his immaturity well into his junior year, and it carried over into his studies.

"Earl was a pretty wild young man in junior high school

and you don't grow out of that overnight," says C. C. Baker, the John Tyler principal who was an assistant principal then. "I think it took a period in his sophomore, junior, and senior years to realize that the demands put on him in the classroom were for his own best interests.

"Earl was an average to poor student. He did graduate with a C average, however. That was good enough to get him in the University of Texas, and he made it on his own."

But not without a struggle. "He was a young man trying to find himself," Baker says. "Like a lot of young people at that time in their lives, he didn't always express it in the best way. To many, he was sullen and hostile. Inwardly, he wasn't that way at all. Earl sometimes was misunderstood in the classroom because of his quietness. Some teachers interpreted this as not being interested or not working."

On the football field, however, there was no misinterpreting his eagerness to play.

"As a linebacker, Earl was something awesome," said David Wells, his old Moore Junior High teammate who played for Tyler's other high school, Robert E. Lee. "He would body-slam a ball carrier. He was so strong he would just pick him off the ground and throw him down. There wasn't a back who could outrun him, so he was all over the field."

Early in his sophomore year Earl gained a new running mate. Like Wells, Lynn King played fullback and linebacker and thrived on an active life—he was president of Future Farmers of America and liked to ride bulls in local rodeos. He admired Earl as an athlete.

King, who is white, had been a rival in junior high. In the eighth grade he played for Boulter against Earl, who was playing for Dogan, and with integration in the ninth grade he transferred to Stewart, previously an all-black school, while Earl moved to Moore, previously all-white. When they were united on the John Tyler B team in 1971, they became friends who would play important roles in the school's climb to the top of Texas high school football.

King and Campbell roomed together on road trips, and King often was the key blocker on Campbell's big runs. (Earl never forgot it; years later, as an all-American in college, he emphasized the great value of teammates who clear the way and recalled his high school days. "Lynn King," he said, "is the reason I am sitting where I am now.")

"By the time we were seniors, Earl and I had been close a long time," King says. "Once they turned him loose as a running back he was terrific. Normally, I blocked—a lot. We ran the Veer and Power I, and the outside sweeps from the Veer were deadly. Earl was strong enough to run over a lot of people and fast enough to outrun a lot of others."

When they were sophomores King helped Earl win a promotion from the B team to the varsity. Nelson brought Lynn up early in the season to play middle linebacker after the regular was injured. Then, after a couple of games, King also was hurt, and Nelson called for Earl although he really wanted to keep him on the B team all season.

"Earl was ready physically to move up," he said, "but not mentally. I didn't think his attitude was what it should be and I felt a full year on the B team would help that. But halfway through the season we hadn't won a game and were about to play Longview without a proven middle linebacker. So I put Earl in there.

"He was just great. Longview tried to throw a lot of dropback passes and Earl sacked the quarterback nine times. We won, 10–7, and decided to keep Earl on the varsity the rest of the year just for defense. We won two more games and tied one, so we finished a 3–6–1 record, a real improvement from midseason."

Earl weighed 195 pounds that season. By the start of his junior year he was over 200, and Nelson planned to use him on offense as well as defense. He felt certain Earl wouldn't wear down playing both ways.

"During our two-a-day practices before school started," he noted, "a lot of hay was being cut, combined, and hauled on the farms out near where Earl lived. The farmers would

come to our workouts, hoping to hire Earl and his brothers
(Tim and Steve were sophomores) to come haul hay. They
had a reputation as great workers, and everyone wanted
them. I finally told the farmers that was fine with me, but
please wait until practice ended. So they used to line up
out there by the practice field, waiting to take them to
haul hay.

"Earl was always a worker. He had all the basic qualities
you want for knowing what it was to be a part of a family
or a team. That was the way he was raised. He had gotten
away from that for a while around school, but he began
to mature as a person between his sophomore and junior
years. He started accepting the fact that he was not something special but just part of the team."

Earl injured an ankle in a preseason scrimmage with
Plano High School, however, and it was so sore that Nelson
decided to limit him to linebacking until midseason. Then
he let him play both ways in the crucial game with
Longview. Although Longview won the game and went
on to win the district title, everyone left the stadium that
night raving about how that big number 20 carried the
ball for John Tyler.

By the day of the final game with crosstown rival Robert
E. Lee, Earl had gained 875 yards rushing. Everyone was
wondering if he could gain enough that night to earn the
unusual distinction of a 1,000-yard season—in half a season. Then Nelson learned Earl hadn't yet outrun his immaturity.

"We had our pep rally during the first period of school,"
Nelson said, "and Earl and four of his teammates decided,
since this was the last game of the year and this was Robert
E. Lee and everybody in town was excited, driving up and
down the streets hollering and cheering, that they'd just
skip school. They came back for the athletic period, the
last period of the day, when the players met with the
coaches and started getting ready for the game, and I didn't
even know they had been gone.

"Then I got word that their teachers had reported them
absent all day. The school district had a rule that if you

didn't attend class the day of a game you weren't eligible
to play in the game that night. I was really mad. All five
of them were starters, and I suspended all of them from
the team. Earl was the only one who had another season
of eligibility, and I told him if he wanted to play his senior
year he had better show me a lot during the off-season.
I told all of them they had been very selfish and thought-
less, not only by jeopardizing their own opportunity to
play but by jeopardizing the team's opportunity to win. I
got so mad I overreacted in some of the things I said,
but I didn't overreact in suspending them from the team.
They deserved that."

Lynn King remembered Nelson telling the rest of the
team that they would be playing without five starters that
night.

"He was really resentful about it," King said. "Then
he called me in and said, 'Lynn, you'll be carrying a lot
tonight. You're going to have to pull us through.' "

Rose Stadium was packed with thirteen thousand fans
that night, despite a freezing rain. "They came to see Earl,"
King chuckled. What they saw instead was a wild, rugged
game, with King trying to blast through a Lee defense
led by David Wells. John Tyler finally won, 7–0, for an
8–2 season record, finishing second to Longview in the
district race.

The Lions weren't highly regarded when the 1973 season opened. They had only three returning starters—
Campbell, King, and quarterback Larry Hartsfield—and
were picked to finish fourth in the district. But a lot of
younger players came through, like linebackers Tim and
Steve Campbell, and with big brother Earl running wild
they started winning. Most of the games were close, but
they always came through, even when Earl was sidelined
in the second quarter of the Nacogdoches game with a
hip pointer, an injury which kept him out of the next two
games. Although Nacogdoches led 7–0 at the time of Earl's
injury, John Tyler rallied to win, 14–7.

Earl scored twenty-eight touchdowns that season, and

Lawrence LaCroix informed him early that he shouldn't stage a show in the end zone after each one.

"Once I did a dance," Earl recalled, "and Coach LaCroix told me it wasn't necessary to do that to get recognized. He said, 'Just play ball as best you can. People are going to see and read about what you do anyway.'

That ended any inclinations to showboat. "The next Friday night I couldn't wait to get in the end zone. When I did, I just handed the ball to the ref."

Earl benefited from good counseling by his coaches, who always knew they had the complete support of his mother. "Mrs. Campbell and I talked a lot about Earl and his goals and his dreams and how he was coming along in developing as a total person," Nelson said. "She was always 100 percent behind the school administration and the coaches. Now she would not stand for anyone abusing Earl, but she was the kind of person who believed that if people cared about you, spent the time trying to communicate with you and trying to discipline you, that was the right way. Earl was without a father, and she knew he was a strong-willed person anyway and he needed strong leadership.

"Earl probably related to Lawrence LaCroix as a father figure, and I think Coach LaCroix did a great job in providing Earl with the proper examples. I think Earl looked on me more as a disciplinarian, a leader, a teacher, and a person who was interested in him."

And as the coach who told him his greatest future in football was as a running back, not a linebacker. "Coach Nelson," Earl said when his career as an NFL runner was soaring, "is one of the people I owe a lot in life."

When the Lions stormed into the state playoffs, they learned that Earl got better as the pressure mounted. He gained a total of 857 yards in five playoff games, including some crucial ground late in the semifinal game with Conroe.

Conroe, ranked No. 1 in Texas at the time, held a 7–3 lead with 2:15 left to play and Tyler needing to drive 88 yards to score a touchdown. But Earl and the Lions kept blasting and made it. After that game, Conroe coach W. T. Stapler sighed heavily. "I always thought Superman was white," he said, "but he's not. He's black, wears number 20, and plays for John Tyler."

The perfect ending came December 22 in the Astrodome, the stadium which would become Earl's home with the Houston Oilers five years later. John Tyler beat Austin Reagan 21–14 for the state championship, with Earl rushing for 164 yards on thirty-two carries and scoring two touchdowns. The players never enjoyed a bus ride home like the one that night.

"We got in about ten," Lynn King recalls, "and Earl said, 'Okay, let's have a party at my house.' Lamar Willis, the team manager, and I went, and we were the only two white guys there. We had a terrific time, let me tell you.

"There must have been forty people in that old house, the family and all their friends. We even had some beer, and Mama didn't fuss about the drinking. I guess she felt it was a special occasion. As well as I remember, Earl didn't drink much, but I know I did."

Earl knew the party was over the next day when he did something that disturbed his mother. "A youngster showed up at their house and asked to see Earl," Corky Nelson says. "He had asked his daddy to drive him out there so he could get Earl's autograph. Earl sent back word he was too tired to visit.

"Mrs. Campbell told Earl that he had accomplished a few things and that with those accomplishments came added responsibilities. One of those was to talk to people and be nice. I think some of Earl's brothers and sisters got on him, too. Earl went out and visited with the kid."

The next day was Christmas Eve and Lynn King took Earl, Tim, and Steve downtown for some shopping. "People were overwhelmed by the state championship and were giving us gifts," he said. "It was wild. We didn't need much money."

The twins had led the team in tackles, collectively holding up their side of the game almost as well as Earl did his. No wonder a new bumper sticker appeared around

Tyler. Its message was simple and sincere: "Thank You, Mrs. Campbell."

And John Tyler High School was a much happier place than it was three years earlier. "I saw a change in race relationships in the school because of Earl Campbell's leadership," says C. C. Baker. "Earl and other blacks did such a fine job on the playing field that the whites were pleased we had such fine athletes representing John Tyler.

"I think that definitely pulled the school together. I'm not naive enough to think we still don't have problems in school between blacks and whites, however. We still need a lot of growth.

"I wish we had some more Earl Campbells to bring it about."

CHOOSING THE LONGHORNS

As Darrell Royal and Ken Dabbs drove away from their hotel that afternoon in Dallas, the weather reminded them of the University of Texas's performance in the Cotton Bowl Classic two days before—cold and dreary. A biting wind and icy roads discouraged travel, but their trip was too important to delay.

Their football season had ended on New Year's Day when Nebraska had beat the Longhorns 19–3, and now came recruiting season, when they could turn this into a happy new year. It was January 3, 1974. Dabbs, Texas's recruiting coordinator, was taking Royal to Tyler for his first visit with Earl Campbell and his mother.

Driving east on Interstate 20, Dabbs nervously watched the speedometer and his watch. He felt encouraged about his earlier visits in the Campbell home. He had enjoyed good rapport with the family, eating chicken at Ann Campbell's table and talking with Earl on the front porch while they chewed Red Man. They had seemed sincerely interested in Texas, but the head coach's visit could be the key.

When they pulled in at that faded old farm house, Dabbs felt relieved. During the hundred-mile trip they had seen seven of those big sixteen-wheel trailer-trucks turned over on the ice.

He felt new tension when they entered the house, however.

Ann Campbell was running a temperature and didn't feel like getting out of bed, but she had told them they were welcome to visit that afternoon. She was polite as they took chairs in her bedroom, but Dabbs noticed that Ann and Earl, so friendly on other occasions, seemed tense and uncomfortable around Royal.

Earl quickly made it clear what was bothering them.

"I understand you don't like black people," he told Royal.

"No, Earl, that's wrong," Royal replied calmly. Then he talked about his feelings toward all human beings and made it clear he had no prejudice.

Royal wasn't surprised to hear Earl suggest he was a racist. The subject had come up for several years now. A lot of people had noticed that Texas's 1969 national championship team was all white, and that the 1970 team which had extended the Longhorns' winning streak to thirty games had included only one black player. A few more blacks had appeared on the roster thereafter, most noticeably all-America fullback Roosevelt Leaks, but Royal still was suspected of being a redneck. He had heard it before and he was prepared when Campbell raised the subject.

"Darrell," says Dabbs, "did a super job of convincing Earl he was a real person and had compassion and warmth for everybody. I guess we stayed two hours, and we did a lot that evening. The atmosphere was cold when we came in but extremely warm when we left."

Royal, with his folksy charm and easy personality, quickly got on the same wave length as Earl and his mother.

"I just asked that they take me for what I am, let me answer questions about myself and the University of Texas, and I'd let folks from other schools have the same privilege," Royal recalls. "I told them I wasn't going to talk about other people, but that I would tell them anything they wanted to know about my thoughts, my feelings, and the University of Texas. I asked simply that they not let other people taint their impressions of me. They seemed to like that attitude. We settled down and had a good, relaxed visit."

As a boy in Oklahoma, Royal had seen his family struggle with poverty during the Dust Bowl days of the thirties. He could identify with the hard times the Campbells had known since Earl's father died in 1966.

"Mrs. Campbell said something about their house," Royal remembers. "It wasn't in an apologetic way, but recognizing the fact that their house wasn't much. I told her the gospel truth. I said, 'Mrs. Campbell, your house looks better than the one I lived in with my grandmother when I was growing up.' Which it really did. It was a better-built house and better furnished than the house I lived in with Grandma Harmon. So we got off pretty good just from that standpoint."

Royal made it clear that Earl would be welcome at Texas on a scholarship, but that he would not be offered anything illegal. Earl knew what he meant—some recruiters had offered him cars, clothes, cash, and help for his mother.

"Earl, if this is a factor, and that is what you want," Royal said, "please don't string me along. Some way or another, let me know you're not interested in us if you're going to go for that kind of a deal."

Earl looked Royal straight in the eye.

"Coach, my people were bought and sold when they didn't have a choice," he said. "Nobody is going to buy Earl."

"Man, that impressed me," Royal recalls. "I knew he had tremendous pride."

The visit ended on a relaxed and friendly note. Royal told Earl he would look forward to his visiting the UT campus at Austin some weekend soon. Dabbs was delighted. He felt they had made real progress. But, realizing that blue-chip high school athletes can be stricken by frequent changes of mood and preferences during the recruiting season, he knew the battle was far from won.

Every other school in the Southwest (and many others

across the country) wanted Earl to be wearing its uniform in the fall of 1974. He heard from a lot of other famous coaches, some of them also quite appealing and convincing. By mid-January Earl was still undecided about his future college, if not about Royal.

"I don't know if I'll go to his school," he said, "but I'll always respect him, not as a football coach but as a person."

Dabbs notes, "Earl and his mother believed and trusted Coach Royal. The big thing he did that day was not only sell the University of Texas but also sell himself. He talked about some of his own experiences when he was young, his experiences as a coach, some of the people he had met. He really touched them."

Earl recalls, "Coach Royal talked about living with his grandma and how he always regretted that she died before he had grown up and was able to help her. That made me even more determined to do something for my mother."

While Royal had made a highly favorable impression, Dabbs developed a close relationship with the Campbells through his repeated visits, and that also was quite valuable.

"They accepted me almost as one of the family," he says. "I would eat dinner with them, and the food was excellent. I've always called Mrs. Campbell the best chicken cook in America. And I enjoyed a special feeling when I was in that house. There was a tremendous amount of warmth, love, and compassion for one another."

Although Ann Campbell believed in the country life, she showed no apprehension about Earl going to UT Austin, a university with more than forty thousand enrollment in a city of more than three hundred thousand. She wanted Earl to make the decision about his college, but Dabbs sensed she really wanted him to stay in the state of Texas.

"We stressed the contacts which could be made through going to the University of Texas," he says. "We stressed it was a two-way street—the University of Texas could help Earl and Earl could help the University of Texas.

"Earl and I became super friends. We'd sit on the front porch or the hood of the car, chewing Red Man, spitting and talking about everything but football. He had his private goals set so high, things he wanted to do for his mother and his family and what he wanted to do with his life. We'd talk about what he needed to do to reach them. Always in the course of the conversation he'd ask me, 'You think I can do that?' I always reassured him that he could."

There were no guarantees of instant stardom, however.

"I told Earl that we felt he was an outstanding talent, as good as we'd seen in years and years," Royal notes, "but that truthfully I couldn't say for sure he'd even be able to make the team.

"I told him I thought we'd been judging talent long enough and were pretty good judges, that we couldn't be all that wrong in our evaluation of him. I told him he'd have to prove himself just like everyone else we recruited, though. I really think Earl liked that approach."

Struggling to graduate from John Tyler High School with a C average, Earl was concerned about making it as a student in college. He didn't just want to attend and stay eligible for football. He wanted to graduate.

"A degree was very important to Earl," Dabbs said. "A lot of people thought he couldn't get a degree. Yet in the back of his mind he believed that if he worked hard and took advantage of his opportunity he could do it."

Earl was interested in a major in speech communication, so Rex Wier, assistant dean in the UT College of Communication, discussed the program with Earl and his mother.

"I said we would do everything we could to help Earl earn his degree," Wier says, "but that we certainly couldn't give him one. If he could pass the course work, we would help him work toward that end."

The Longhorns grew larger in Earl's mind as the weeks passed and the February date for signing the Southwest Conference letter of intent neared. He also visited Baylor, the world's largest Baptist university, and was impressed with the Bears' head coach, Grant Teaff, and assistant Bill Lane, who also recruited him extensively. He cancelled a weekend visit to the University of Houston, however, and made the Longhorns' winter, summer, spring, and fall by announcing he would sign with Texas.

Why did he select Texas from the dozens of schools which wanted him?

"I liked what I saw, what I heard, and what I was getting," he says. "The campus looked beautiful, and the people were friendly. They offered to help me get an education. Texas did not buy me. Blacks are through selling themselves, or at least I'm not going to sell myself. Texas offered me everything legal, and there was none of this stupid talk of cars."

(Earl, in fact, did not own a car until his senior year at Texas. He bought a '67 Oldsmobile for three hundred dollars from a man in Tyler, and proudly referred to it as "my Rolls.")

On the night before the Southwest Conference signing day, Royal and Dabbs returned to Tyler, spent the night at the Ramada Inn, and were at the Campbell house by seven-thirty in the morning. The place was aglow, filled with family, friends, and Earl's high school coaches.

"We had our coffee and got our visiting done before signing time," Royal says. "At eight o'clock I handed Earl my pen and we signed that dude. We shook hands and I jumped in the car and headed for the airplane. We had a pretty good day signing guys like Gralyn Wyatt and Alfred Jackson, players who would help a lot the next four years, and Earl kicked it off for us."

A week later, Dabbs returned and signed Earl to the national letter of intent, thus preventing any school outside the SWC from luring Campbell away from Texas. There really was no chance of that by then, although Earl had upset Royal several weeks earlier when he insisted on visiting the University of Oklahoma, which consistently built its national powerhouses with blue-chip players from Texas.

"I came on pretty strong about it," says Royal, whose '73 Longhorn team had taken a 52–13 licking from the Sooners under their new head coach, Barry Switzer. "I said, 'Earl, you told us you were coming and I kinda thought that meant you wouldn't be visiting other places.' He bowed right up. 'I gave you my word,' he said, 'but I do want to go up there and see that school. I've heard a lot about it.' "

Campbell was greatly impressed by Oklahoma, so much so that he had second thoughts about his decision. As he knelt beside his bed one night to pray, he said, "Lord, if I am supposed to go to Texas, arouse me during the night."

He awoke in the middle of the night.

"If I hadn't been aroused," Earl says, "I probably would have gone to Oklahoma."

Three years later, when Earl was a junior and Royal was taking the Longhorns into his final game against Oklahoma before retiring from coaching, they sat together on the bus that was carrying the team from its Dallas hotel to the Cotton Bowl.

"Earl, if you hadn't given me your word," Royal asked, "do you think you would have gone to Oklahoma?"

"Close," Earl said.

BIG MOMENTS— AND MISERY

AUSTIN ENJOYS A SPECIAL DISTINCTION among the cities of Texas. As the state capital and the home of the main campus of the University of Texas, its blend of government, politics, education, and athletics creates a vibrant and appealing atmosphere. Located among the hills and lakes of Central Texas, Austin is blessed with pretty scenery and friendly people, and country music fills the air. It's a town that's easy to take.

Earl Campbell learned that quickly when he reported for football practice at Texas in late summer of 1974, but he still felt homesick. Thinking of his mother, family, and girlfriend, many evenings he would sit on the curb outside his dormitory, listen to the chimes in the UT Tower, and face in the direction of Tyler. Somehow this seemed to bring them closer.

It was simply the period of adjustment which so many college freshmen go through when they leave home. Earl was an exceptional football prospect, but this didn't make him immune to the common malady.

After a couple of weeks however, he was doing fine.

The first Sunday he had not attended church because he didn't know where to go. The second Sunday he began worshiping regularly at Mount Olive Baptist Church in East Austin. The only other Sunday he missed church his first year was in late December, when the Longhorns were in Florida for the Gator Bowl.

The ease with which he settled into his new life was a pleasant surprise to him. He originally had felt that Austin would be a place to go to college for four years, play football, and no more.

"When I got there," Earl says, "I saw things differently. People were friendly and a lot nicer than I expected. I couldn't wait to go back to Tyler to tell Mama how good it really was. I didn't want to go back to stay, just to tell Mama."

Belonging to the Texas football team gave him a good sensation, too.

"I wondered if I would have pride in my team and my school as I did in high school," he said that first year. "I found that I have more pride. There is competition here. I admire Roosevelt Leaks because he made me work."

Leaks, an all-America fullback as a junior in 1973, reported for his senior season after knee surgery. He was determined to play, although he could have stayed out of competition that fall, rehabilitated the knee further, and completed his eligibility in 1975. The Longhorns ran the Wishbone offense, which made the fullback a heavy-duty ball carrier, and Texas coach Darrell Royal had Campbell, now 220 pounds, playing there from the first practice. Leaks didn't regain the form of his junior season, but he worked hard and pushed Earl to learn a new offense and position.

When the fall semester began, Earl attended his classes as faithfully as football practice. Just before enrolling he had said, "I wonder if I can really make the grades? The day school starts, I'll start studying. I pray nothing gets in my way to keep me from studying."

As the semester progressed, he explained, "Look, I know I'm not the smartest person, and I know I don't work on my studies as hard at times as I should. I do know you should go to class and be interested.

"If you put forth the effort to show up for a class every day, it shows that professor you're interested in getting an education. If at the end you're on the borderline, that professor is going to remember that he's seen your face there all the time. He'll know you've been trying. It's got to help."

Realistically, Earl didn't expect to become an academic all-American, but he set extremely high goals for himself in football. Consider a paper he wrote for an introductory communications class:

"Before I leave, I want to gain 2,000 yards in one season, win the Heisman Trophy, be on a national championship team and help us win the Southwest Conference the next three years. Then I want to turn pro and sign for enough money to buy Mama a new house."

Had he seen that paper, Royal probably would have whistled softly and exclaimed, "Way to go, Earl!"

From the start, Royal felt Earl was an outstanding prospect for major college football. By the time he watched Earl in a few early scrimmages he privately upgraded his appraisal.

"Earl was good enough as a freshman to go into pro football," Royal declared a few years later. "I'm not saying he would have been a star immediately. He wasn't ready to play, but no one would have had enough guts to cut him and let him go somewhere else for seasoning, because you could see the raw talent there."

A young player like Earl had to excite Royal as he prepared for his eighteenth season as Texas's head coach. In 1957, when he took charge of the then-lowly Longhorns, Royal had been thirty-three, and determined to earn a place among the game's leaders. He had done that and more, and his knack for expressing himself in the down-to-earth manner he grew up with in the little town of Hollis, Oklahoma, had been as impressive as his record.

Once injuries had wiped out his best punters, leaving a glaring weakness on an otherwise excellent team. Finally a replacement had been found—on the track team. The kid had kicked the ball weakly, but he had managed to avoid getting it blocked, and Royal had let him punt most of the season.

When someone had mentioned how ordinary Texas's punting was compared to other phases of its game, Royal had pointed out that sometimes looks aren't everything.

"Ol' Ugly," he had said, "is better than Ol' Nuthin'."

Before his first season Royal had declared he was looking for highly-motivated players, the type to compete fiercely against Oklahoma, the toughest Southwest Conference rivals, and other national powers.

"We need guys," he had said, "who'll dance every dance."

Through the years Royal had had more dancing partners than Fred Astaire, becoming the winningest coach in SWC history. When Campbell became a Longhorn, Royal's teams had won seven league titles and tied for three more in seventeen years, had had perfect-record, national championship seasons in 1963 and 1969, and had once won thirty straight games. Royal had been widely acclaimed for these achievements, being voted national Coach of the Year three times and selected Coach of the Decade for the 1960s by ABC Television.

He loved to play golf and listen to country and western music. During the later stages of his coaching career he had received considerable publicity, and some criticism, for his friendships with such famous singers as Charley Pride, Willie Nelson and Johnny Rodriguez.

Some suggested Royal had grown soft from success and didn't want to work as hard as he once had to keep Texas among the national powers. True, the annual grudge game with the University of Oklahoma, where Royal had been an all-America quarterback for Bud Wilkinson in 1949, had swung back in the Sooners' favor. Oklahoma had beaten Texas three straight years, the most recent being the 52–13 embarrassment in Barry Switzer's first year as head coach. Previously Royal's teams had won twelve of thirteen games from 1958 through 1970.

Now, at fifty, Royal would have delighted in building one more Longhorn powerhouse, proving he could do it in the '70s as well as he had done in the '60s. In the fall of '74, it was difficult to foresee if Royal might eventually do it, but it was obvious he had the cornerstone for any job in the muscular body of Earl Campbell.

Playing fullback in the Wishbone formation, lined up two yards behind the quarterback and one step up from the halfbacks, Campbell was the key to Royal's offense, which placed a premium on strong running. The Wishbone quarterback either handed the ball to the fullback or faked it, then sprinted to the outside like he had the ball—whether he kept it or not—with a halfback trailing him for a possible pitchback. Meanwhile, the fullback tore into the heart of the defense, trying to find daylight if he had the ball or trying to attract a crowd if he didn't. Campbell had played halfback in high school, running outside frequently, but he adjusted quickly to the demands of his new position.

He exploded on some long runs in pre-season scrimmages, and Royal was pleased.

"Freshman or not, Campbell is an outstanding football player," he said. "He's got a lot of tools to work with, and when he gets pointed in the right direction he's pointed with authority."

Still, he was a nineteen-year-old freshman. Earl wasn't set, nor was the team. When the season opened it was obvious that Texas, while not a national power, could be dangerous against any opponent when it was playing its best. And when it wasn't, it might struggle to beat a weaker team or look bad losing to a good one.

The Longhorns did the latter against Texas Tech, taking a 26–3 licking which made them seem a soft touch for mighty Oklahoma a couple of weeks later. Before facing the Sooners, they played a so-so Washington team, moving the ball freely but also yielding a lot in a 35–21 victory. That same Saturday night in Memorial Stadium the Texas fans saw Earl's first big performance; he rushed 125 yards on sixteen carries, scored a touchdown, and once broke for 36 yards. Everyone was aware, however, that it wasn't the Oklahoma defense he was tearing through.

The Sooners took a whirlwind offense as well as a savage defense to Dallas for the annual State Fair of Texas battle. They were ranked No. 2 nationally and favored by three to four touchdowns. The Longhorns, stung by the memory of their 52–13 whipping the year before, came up from Austin with a bad disposition and new ammunition. Royal was quietly confident.

"We're ready to get after 'em," he said.

Came the kickoff and they did. The Sooners squeezed out a 7–3 halftime lead but Texas, alert and aggressive, pulled ahead in a big third quarter. Earl's 12-yard touchdown burst gave the Longhorns a 10–7 lead. A field goal a few minutes later made the score 13–7.

Oklahoma found itself fighting to come back in the fourth quarter against a team nearly everyone thought would be far behind by then. A touchdown made it 13–13 but the tie remained when the conversion kick sailed wide. Texas, with fresh inspiration, started banging into that strong-armed defense again.

At midfield the Longhorns faced fourth down, needing two feet for a first. With nine minutes left Royal might have called for a punt and possibly put the Sooners deep in their end of the field, leaving it to his defense to get the ball back for another shot. But he decided to keep on bucking.

Earl blasted into the middle and made the first down by a foot or so but lost the ball to the Sooners in a tremendous collision. From there Oklahoma moved close enough to kick a field goal and win, 16–13.

Earl's first major test of his college career was a valuable, and realistic, experience. He fumbled on a crucial play, but he also gave the Texas offense new punch that commanded respect. He gained 70 yards on fifteen carries and proved he could run against the toughest opposition.

Earl and the Longhorns returned to Austin with new pride. Everyone was eager to see what they would do next. In a nationally televised game with Arkansas at Memorial

Stadium, the Razorbacks learned they were ready to do a lot, once Earl ignited them.

"That probably was Earl's greatest job of turning a game around for us," Royal notes. "It was a pretty tight ball game, and we were leading 3–0 just before halftime, when he jumped in there with a handoff and went 68 yards for a touchdown. We kicked off, backed 'em up, he goes in and blocks a punt and we got another touchdown. Bam! Suddenly it was 17–0."

Texas won the game 38–7, and Earl wound up with 109 yards rushing on just eight carries. What excited the Longhorns more than his running, however, was the way he streaked in through the middle of the line and blocked the punt. Tackle Doug English grabbed the bouncing ball and rumbled into the end zone while Earl jumped with jubilation behind him.

It looked like Texas had another great weapon—Earl Campbell, blocking punts.

"That showed you how smart we are," Royal mused in later years. "We quit doing it. He got the first one he ever went after and then attempted only two or three more."

There was no easing off for Earl Campbell the runner. He finished the regular season with a rousing performance in cold, rainy Memorial Stadium, blasting out 127 yards on twenty-eight carries as the Longhorns blew Texas A&M out of the SWC championship picture, 32–3.

Texas had suffered its second league loss in a wild 34–24 battle with Baylor, the eventual champion, and was winding up the season with a 5–2 SWC record, 8–3 for the full season, and an invitation to play Auburn in the Gator Bowl. But the Longhorns totally frustrated the Aggies, their traditional rivals, and delighted in raining on their parade. If the Aggies had won they would have tied Baylor with a 6–1 record and gone to the Cotton Bowl. Instead, they got nothing.

At that moment the season seemed a smashing success to the Longhorns and their rare freshman fullback.

"I'll never forget what happened in the locker room,"

offensive tackle Bob Simmons said. "Coach Royal made his little talk and Earl asked if he could say something. He got up on a bench and asked for silence. I thought, 'Here comes a rah-rah, gung-ho speech.' He suddenly struck a silly pose and yelled, 'Ain't I cute? Ain't I cute?' It broke everyone up."

Earl's opening act in college football had been pretty good, too. He had gained 928 yards on 162 carries, scored six touchdowns, and made the all-Southwest Conference team. The future was full of promise for the team and for Earl—everyone would be more poised and experienced in '75. But there was no reason to be overconfident. A 27–3 defeat by Auburn in the Gator Bowl told the Longhorns they had plenty of work ahead.

When it was time for spring practice, Earl felt very comfortable at Texas.

"Last year was a great one for me," he said, "and not just because of football. I wondered how it would be, getting out on my own, but it has made a better man of me. You learn when you get away from home. You have to make sacrifices. The big thing is you learn to communicate with people. That's something I've done."

Royal thought Earl adjusted well to the demands of a big university and big-time college football.

"Other than being homesick, I don't think he had any problems," he said. "Earl has the ability to get along with people, and he's well liked. If something is bothering him he won't keep it in. He'll find somebody he trusts and can visit with and just talk it out."

Earl, it seems, never will make the all-ulcer team.

The best news Ann Campbell heard about Earl's sophomore year wasn't that he was selected for the Coaches' all-America team. It was that he had been kicked out of an Austin night club.

His girlfriend, Reuna Smith, was visiting for the weekend from Tyler, so they went to a club and ordered orange juice. After three glasses, the waitress spoke softly to Earl.

"Sir," she said, "I'm sorry, but the manager has asked us to suggest to people that they leave after a while if they aren't drinking alcoholic beverages."

Earl shrugged it off.

"Only reason I was in there in the first place," he said, "was because Reuna was in town and wanted to see a little night life. Well, we did."

His mother was delighted to hear about it. Since Earl left home for college she had worried about his being swayed by the bright lights, going out for booze instead of staying in with his books.

"That story tickled me," she said, "because it told me Earl was keeping his head. I'd been worrying for no cause."

Aside from that night club, Austin seemed more like home to Earl all the time. His twin brothers, Tim and Steve, were freshmen on the Longhorn squad, and it was good to have them living in Jester Center, the dorm where the athletes were housed. Tim became an immediate asset to the defense at end, becoming the team's best pass rusher in '75. Steve, slowed by a knee injury suffered his senior year at John Tyler High School, worked hard at linebacker but did not play.

Earl was more experienced and confident for his sophomore season, as was the team. Longhorn fans were optimistic when fall practice began and their optimism soared after Texas tore through Colorado State, Washington, Texas Tech, and Utah State by a combined score of 177–35. Earl and Marty Akins, a splendid Wishbone quarterback, fueled the offense and, while the defense was not as strong, it looked tough enough. This could be the Longhorn's best team since 1970, the last time they had beaten Oklahoma.

Earl opened with three straight 100-plus games against Colorado State (103 yards on thirteen carries), Washington (198 on twenty-seven), and Texas Tech (150 on eighteen), before playing sparingly in the 61–7 rout of Utah State. If he was to get a breather, now was the time. Earl would have to go full throttle against Oklahoma.

After proving surprisingly tough for the Sooners in '74, Royal intensified the Longhorns' preparations for this meeting. To him, it had become more than a game.

Stung by Oklahoma's repeated success in recruiting blue-chip Texas high school players, Royal naturally longed to get this rivalry back on his terms. The Sooners were ending a two-year NCAA probation for recruiting violations, but this had not deterred their recruiting in Texas. Soon they would be allowed back on television and in bowl games. This would be an ideal time for a Texas victory.

Royal had championed the use of polygraph tests in investigating suspected recruiting violations, and the Southwest Conference had sanctioned them in the winter of 1974. Shortly before this, Oklahoma coach Barry Switzer had called an Associated Press writer in New York and strongly endorsed the polygraph idea. Royal had promptly said he would be glad to take his staff anywhere to take a lie detector test along with Switzer's Oklahoma staff and have the results published. Switzer had also said he was willing but hadn't finalized it with Royal, and the head-to-head tests were never held. Royal and Switzer had each had their staffs tested privately and nothing more had been said for then.

In the summer of 1975 Switzer had aimed a needle at Royal during a speech to an alumni group. The subject had been the NCAA economy proposals to cut coaching staffs to eight assistants and limit recruiting visits.

"Some coaches don't want to coach any more," Switzer had said. "They would rather sit home and listen to guitar pickers. They want to make it where you can't outwork anybody."

If Royal needed more incentive to prepare for the Oklahoma game, that was it. But wanting it and winning it again proved different matters.

Earl emerged as the top ground gainer in a torrid afternoon in the Cotton Bowl, crashing the Big Red for 95 yards on twenty-three carries, but the runner remembered best was Sooner fullback Horace Ivory. He bolted 33 yards for a touchdown with less than six minutes left in the game, and second-ranked Oklahoma beat fifth-ranked Texas, 24–17.

The Longhorns' orange jerseys darkened from sweat quickly and their fumbles helped stake the Sooners to a 10–0 lead in the first quarter. In the third quarter, Campbell appeared to be down when he was stripped of the ball, but officials ruled another Sooner recovery. This led to a touchdown for a 17–7 lead. Texas countered with a touchdown and then a field goal to make it 17–17 but, as the year before, this only built the Longhorns up for a letdown. Ivory's last-minute charge broke the tie and dashed the Longhorn's hopes of breaking the Oklahoma winning streak.

For the next few weeks, Earl and his teammates settled down to their pursuit of the Southwest Conference title, and in the process he closed in on a 1,000-yard rushing season. When Texas beat Baylor, 37–21, for a 5–0 league record, Earl gained 133 yards for a season total of 1,037 yards, with Texas Christian University and Texas A&M remaining to be played. He was averaging slightly more than 115 yards per game, and the total seemed likely to approach 1,400 for the eleven-game schedule.

Then Earl and the offense hit the skids. Akins suffered a sprained knee early in the TCU game and was carried off with Texas leading 14–0. Royal had said Akins and Campbell were the only two players they couldn't replace, and that was apparent after the senior quarterback left. Freshman Ted Constanzo couldn't maintain the early momentum, and the offense dragged noticeably as Texas won, 27–11, over a team which had lost twenty straight games. Earl gained only 41 yards on nine carries.

Texas, ranked No. 5 and leading the nation in scoring with 35.3 points per game, had thirteen days to prepare to play Texas A&M at College Station the day after Thanksgiving. If the Longhorns won, they would return to the Cotton Bowl on New Year's Day with a 7–0 SWC record. But the Aggies, ranked No. 2 nationally, had a 9–0 season record, with a closing SWC game at Arkansas eight days after the Texas battle. One of those goals Earl had declared early in his freshman year was within reach, but the chance of winning it was shaky because of Akins's injury.

Akins received clearance to play just before the game, but he lasted only ten plays before his knee buckled. If he had been sound, the awesome Aggie defense might have been too much, but without him Texas's offense was almost punchless. There was no versatility to the attack, and the Aggies swarmed Earl repeatedly, limiting him to 40 yards on fifteen carries.

Royal still had some players who wanted to dance every dance, but in that game the music always sounded like the "Aggie War Hymn." A&M won, 20–10, but then blew a perfect season and a Cotton Bowl berth in a 31–6 loss to Arkansas a week later.

This caused a three-way tie for the championship between Arkansas, which played in the Cotton Bowl; A&M, which played in the Liberty Bowl; and Texas, which played in the Astro-Bluebonnet Bowl. It wasn't what Texas had hoped for, but it was much better than the Longhorns expected that afternoon when they limped away from Kyle Field at College Station.

Their trip to Houston to play Colorado on December 28 proved that the Astrodome still held some charm for Earl. Two years earlier he had led John Tyler to a state high school championship there. This time he sparked the Texas offense in a 38–21 victory in the Astro-Bluebonnet Bowl.

Akins was able to play the entire game, and that made a great difference against a massive Colorado defense. Earl, occasionally running from halfback in an offense revised to limit Akins's movement, rushed for 95 yards on nineteen carries and was voted the game's most valuable offensive player. Younger brother Tim, who blocked a punt in the third quarter and recovered it for a touchdown to swing the momentum in Texas's favor, played brilliantly at defensive end and was voted the game's most valuable defensive player.

But in the jubilant locker room Royal had another candidate for special honors. Asked whom he considered the game's most valuable contributor, he said, "I would like to put in a vote for Ann Campbell."

The bowl victory gave Texas a 10–2 record for Earl's sophomore season. He had proved himself one of college football's best runners, gaining 1,118 yards on 198 carries in the regular season and scoring thirteen touchdowns. Add his bowl yardage, and he rushed for a total of 1,213 yards on 217 carries, and made the American Football Coaches Association's all-America team.

Thanks to the bowl game, the Longhorns finished the year on an upbeat. Their jubilation after that victory was a distinct contrast to the outlook that dismal day at A&M, but Earl realized there are going to be some downers in life. "If it weren't for the dark days," he said, "we wouldn't know what it is to walk in the light."

In the year ahead, however, he would have to tell himself that a lot more than he expected.

Earl began spring practice in 1976 running a 40-yard dash. He ended it there, too.

He pulled a hamstring in his right leg and hobbled off to the trainer's room in Memorial Stadium. He couldn't work out that spring, and still had to exercise cautiously when he went home to Tyler that summer. He lived with a sister in town and had a job loading trucks at a warehouse for $2.60 per hour. He didn't get rich but he did get heavy.

Unable to do the full summer conditioning program, he had gained weight and ballooned to over 240 pounds when he returned to Austin for fall workouts. That pulled hamstring kept him upset and puzzled. It was an omen of the type of season it would be for Earl, the Longhorns, and their coach.

"I kept reinjuring it," he said. "I'd never been hurt like that before, so I didn't know how it was supposed to feel. I'd go out and push myself too soon and hurt it again."

Royal already had a big headache with the offense because he didn't have a good replacement at quarterback for the graduated Marty Akins. Now with his superstar hobbling and his status in doubt almost daily, he expected little from the offense in the opener at Boston College.

Little is what he got, too. Earl ran only five times for 23 yards before limping off, and underdog Boston College scored a 14–13 upset.

For the next five games Earl managed to play but he wasn't the same ol' Campbell, not even in the home opener with North Texas State when he gained 208 yards on thirty-two carries in a nervous 17–14 win. It was his first 200-yard performance as a Longhorn, but he wasn't going full speed. He broke loose on an 83-yard run but he limped, trying to avoid stretching his ailing leg, and was tackled on the 4-yard line.

"He wasn't the old slashing, quick Earl he's been," Royal said. "He was running under wraps but he was still out-standing."

Earl kept playing, hoping to overcome his injury, and as the weeks passed he felt better. In a bruising defensive battle with Oklahoma he was the only real weapon in Texas's limited offense, blasting out 91 yards on twenty-seven carries. His total would have surpassed 100 yards easily, but referee Bill Jennings, a Big Eight Conference official, called five motion penalties as coaches and players on the Oklahoma sideline kept yelling that Campbell was starting too quickly.

It was, literally and figuratively, a day when nobody won. Texas had to settle for a 6–6 tie when Oklahoma recovered a fumble late in the game and drove 37 yards for a touchdown in the Sooners' only show of offense. Oklahoma had to settle for it after the touchdown when the holder muffed the snap from center, preventing a kick for the possible winning point.

And Royal was booed by thousands of Oklahoma fans on national television as he walked across the floor of the Cotton Bowl with President Gerald Ford and Switzer for a pregame ceremony. The booers were mad because the day before Royal had accused the Oklahoma coaching staff of receiving information from a spy who secretly watched Texas practices before the Texas-OU game in previous years.

After the game, Royal felt sick as he headed for the locker room. His stomach churned, not only because of the booing but because the Sooners had gotten off the hook when they appeared beaten. And he had some apologizing to do. The day before he had called the Oklahoma coaches "sorry bastards." He thought he had made the comment off the record following an interview with an Associated Press writer, but it was carried all over the country. He publicly regretted the name-calling, but he stuck by his spying charges, and said he would "quit coaching" if Switzer or defensive coordinator Larry Lacewell could pass a polygraph test on the subject. He identified the spy as Lonnie Williams, who once coached with Lacewell at Wichita State. Lacewell later admitted he knew Williams well, but denied the spying.

Almost two years later, when Lacewell had left Switzer's staff, he called Royal in Austin, admitted the spying charges were true and apologized. If he had said it the day of that 6–6 tie, it might have saved Royal a bellyache. Or, considering how that season went, maybe it wouldn't have.

Royal's troubles grew worse a couple of weeks later at Texas Tech. Earl, finally feeling his right leg was sound again, ripped for 65 yards on seven carries in the first quarter, and the Longhorn offense looked better than it had all season. Then he pulled the hamstring in his *left* leg and went to the sideline to watch Tech pull out a 31–28 victory.

In the next few weeks a bumper sticker appeared frequently around Austin: *Unleash Earl!* Royal wished he could, for the team was punchless without him.

The University of Houston, playing its first season in the Southwest Conference race, came to Austin and licked the Longhorns, 30–0, the first Texas loss in Memorial Stadium in forty-three games. Earl watched and winced.

November was hard to endure. Baylor and Texas A&M also beat Texas thoroughly. Campbell couldn't play and had to work out gingerly. Each day the press asked him about his leg, but he didn't know what to say. Some people suggested he was dogging it. Earl's faith in himself was being tested and he sometimes asked himself if he had reached the end of the line.

"I think maybe I learned I was a weak man in some ways," he recalled of that period. "I wanted everything to go my way and, of course, it didn't and I got disgusted. I felt sorry for myself, got down on myself. There were mornings when I hated to see daylight."

Earl became quiet and withdrawn. Fortunately, he had a roommate who supported him and encouraged him when he felt low. James (Sugar Bear) Yates didn't try to give Earl false hope. Instead, he put the problem in perspective.

"There is a next year," Yates reassured him, "and it's not tomorrow."

And he received encouragement from a youngster at Mount Olive Baptist Church who gave him a small plaque inscribed with these words: "Keep Me Going, Lord." He put it on the wall of his room.

While Earl struggled with pain and discouragement Royal quietly decided to retire from coaching at the end of the season, his twentieth at Texas and his twenty-third as a head coach. He would remain as athletic director at Texas. But he was weary of coaching, and even more of the recruiting ratrace and trying to compete with coaches and alumni who broke the rules. He would make his decision public after the closing game with Arkansas in Memorial Stadium on Saturday night, December 4. Ironically, his foremost coaching rival and good friend Frank Broyles had decided to retire from his Arkansas job at the same time.

Earl wanted badly to play in that last game, although he wasn't certain of his leg. But following pregame warmup he told Royal he could play, and the mood of the evening picked up noticeably.

Earl made up for some of those missing weeks and the misery, rushing for 131 yards on twenty-seven carries and scoring two touchdowns in a 27–12 victory, giving him a total of 653 yards on 138 carries for the seven games in which he had played that season. The game was nationally televised, and at the final gun Royal and Broyles shook hands as coaching rivals for the last time, then headed for the locker rooms to talk to their teams. Royal didn't have to walk. As the crowd of fifty thousand gave him a standing ovation he was carried from the field on the shoulders of his players.

Earl was glad he could be part of his coach's farewell, for his sake as well as Royal's.

"I learned something about myself in that game," he said. "I learned that ol' Earl had more inside him than even I thought was there. That is when I realized you have to push yourself harder and give a little more."

The victory pulled Texas even at the end of the troubled season with a 5–5–1 record, assuring Royal of never having a sub-.500 season at Texas. He retired at the age of fifty-two with a twenty-year record of 166 wins, 46 losses, and 4 ties for a winning percentage of .778. He had a lot of thrills, but he had decided it was time "to set my bucket down."

Ann Campbell remembers how she sat in front of her TV set that night and cried when she saw Royal at the end of the game. In the jam-packed Texas locker room Earl saw Royal surrounded by reporters, so he stood on a chair in the back of the room and waved at his coach. Royal, looking relieved and happy after weeks of pressure, smiled and waved back. Then Earl squeezed through the crowd to shake his hand.

"Coach Royal is one of those guys you can never measure the depth of," he said. "He just goes on and on."

PHOTO: Tyler *Courier-Times Telegraph*

Tyler, Texas—famous for roses, oil, and Earl Campbell.
Above: On Earl Campbell Day, the whole city turned out
to honor its hometown hero. *Below:* The "old house" where
Earl grew up. One of the first things he did as a pro was
to buy a new house for his mother.

PHOTO: Eliot Kamenitz, Dallas *Morning News*

PHOTO: David Woo, Dallas *Morning News*

Ann Campbell and grandson Victor on porch of the old home.

PHOTO: Tyler *Courier-Times Telegraph*

Above: On the day his high school jersey number (20) was retired, Earl posed with high school head coach Corky Nelson (left) and junior high head coach Lawrence La Croix (right). *Right:* Earl Christian Campbell with Earl Christian Kinzie, the doctor who delivered him and gave him his name.

PHOTO: Shelly Katz

On Campus—the University of Texas.
Left: Earl signs an autograph for a fellow student. *Below:* A family gathering in Earl's dormitory room. Earl and his brother Tim (also a player for UT) are shirtless; others are baby brother Ronnie, Mama, and baby sister Margaret.

PHOTO: Shelly Katz

Moving toward the Heisman. *Top:* November 1977. Earl backs into the end zone for a touchdown against Texas A&M. *Middle:* Earl with tackler George James (#79) and quarterback Randy McEachern (#6) after the 4-touchdown, 282-yard game with A&M, the final game before the Heisman. *Bottom:* Earl's famous touchdown run against Oklahoma in October 1977. Earl swerves past teammate Steve Hall's key block for a 24-yard touchdown run.

PHOTOS THIS PAGE: David Woo, Dallas
Morning News

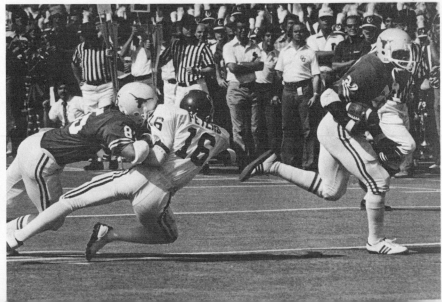

PHOTOS THIS PAGE: University of Texas Sports News Service

Former UT head coach Darrell Royal and Earl Campbell give "Hook 'Em" sign during ceremonies retiring Earl's University of Texas jersey number (20).

Earl with his mother and UT head coach Fred Akers at the Heisman Trophy dinner in New York City—1977.

Entering Oiler Country. Earl Campbell at Press Conference
after the Houston Oilers drafted him No. 1 in the NFL draft
of 1978. On far left are Ann Campbell and Oiler head coach
Bum Phillips.

Houston fans show their affection for Earl Campbell at a "Monday Night
Football" game against Pittsburgh in the Astrodome.

PHOTO: Lou Witt

Opposite page: Earl, after taking handoff from quarterback Dan Pastorini, looks for opening against the Pittsburgh Steelers

Right: Earl breaks open behind strong Oiler blocking against the Cleveland Browns (September 1979).

PHOTO: David Woo, Dallas *Morning News*

Above: Earl's 71-yard run against Dallas on Thanksgiving Day, 1979. Earl sprints away from diving Cowboy defender Aaron Kyle; Oiler teammate Rob Carpenter at far right. *Left:* Earl dodges Pittsburgh linebacker Jack Lambert.

PHOTO: Lou Witt

PHOTO: Eliot Kamenitz, Dallas *Morning News*

The New House. *Above:* Ann Campbell relaxes in the living room of her new home with "her" Heisman Trophy. *Below:* Ann stands with granddaughter, Nadia, in front of the new antique brick house.

PHOTO: Eliot Kamenitz, Dallas *Morning News*

PHOTO: Jim Harrison

In May 1980, Earl married the one true love of his life, Reuna Smith.

NEXT PAGE PHOTO: Lou Witt

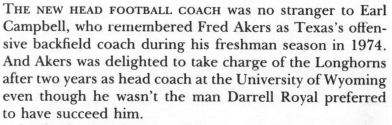

THAT PERFECT AUTUMN 7

THE NEW HEAD FOOTBALL COACH was no stranger to Earl Campbell, who remembered Fred Akers as Texas's offensive backfield coach during his freshman season in 1974. And Akers was delighted to take charge of the Longhorns after two years as head coach at the University of Wyoming even though he wasn't the man Darrell Royal preferred to have succeed him.

Strangely, Royal was snubbed in the selection process. The chairman of the UT Board of Regents, former governor Allan Shivers, named a blue-ribbon selection committee of seven persons that didn't include Royal. Despite his experience as a highly successful coach and the fact that he remained athletic director, Royal would have no real voice in picking his successor and that weakened his recommendation of Mike Campbell for the job.

A Longhorn assistant throughout Royal's twenty years as head coach, Mike Campbell was widely respected for his keen football mind. He was assistant head coach and chief defensive coach, had contributed greatly to Texas's success and Royal believed he was ideally qualified to move up. Mike was fifty-four years old and the committee may have felt that was quite late in a career for a guy to embark on his first college head coaching job no matter how much authority he held during Royal's regime. What seemed to hurt him more, however, was his close association with Royal.

The committee was chaired by Dr. Lorene Rogers, president of UT Austin, but Shivers also was a member and evidently exercised a strong voice. It was said that Shivers and other influential people were annoyed by Royal's casual lifestyle in recent years and his friendships with famous country singers, who sometimes were Darrell's guests on the sidelines during games. But whatever the reasons, the committee wanted a coach with a different image.

Akers was that. Bright, handsome and impressively dressed in well-tailored three-piece suits, Akers could be cordial yet businesslike. He generated ambition and energy. At thirty-eight he was not too old and not too young, and although he had spent nine years as an assistant on Royal's staff he and Royal never had been particularly close.

The committee was impressed by the fact that Frank Broyles, for whom Akers had played at Arkansas in the late '50s, spoke highly of Akers, and that Fred was a top candidate for the Razorback job. Broyles, like Royal, remained as athletic director after his retirement from coaching but, unlike Royal, had complete authority in hiring his successor. When he landed his first choice, New York Jets coach Lou Holtz, the UT committee made a strong move for Akers.

On December 15, 1976, eleven days after Royal received a standing ovation in Memorial Stadium and was carried from the field on his players' shoulders and shortly before Dr. Rogers's announcement to the press, he was informed that Akers would succeed him.

Earl Campbell has remained tremendously fond of Royal, saying that after his retirement from coaching they developed a father-son relationship. But he also appreciated Akers's coaching talent, the way he motivated players and the role he played in Earl's spectacular senior season. He respected both of his college coaches but realized they were two different men.

Earl, delighted by the Longhorns' revitalization under Akers, said, "I won't make any comparisons between coach Royal and coach Akers because I didn't know coach Royal when he was thirty-eight years old."

Akers, of course, took charge after the worst year of Royal's Texas career, and the atmosphere was ripe for change. He made a strong impression in his first team meeting.

"He told us," Earl recalls, "we could keep doing the same things losers do and we could have another 5–5–1 season if we wanted."

Akers believed he must reinstill pride in the program, which he felt had dwindled in the last four or five years, and he told the players he would be talking to them one-on-one and help them establish personal goals. He knew that there was good material at this school, with its rich football tradition, and he was determined to mold it in his own fashion and make it productive.

"When you have competitors like we've got," Akers said, "you challenge them. When they meet one challenge, you give them another and another, and just keep going."

Akers thrived on challenges. He was always an achiever as a youngster in Blytheville, Arkansas, the only one of nine children to finish high school. The family was poor, and Fred learned early about the necessity of hard work. He mowed lawns and hoed and picked cotton. How much cotton did he pick?

"Enough to last me the rest of my life," he says.

When he was in the fifth grade he benefited from the guidance of Mitchell Johns, a family friend and junior high teacher who provided clothing and taught him to appreciate the cultural life. A valuable relationship began. After Akers entered the University of Arkansas, Johns moved there as a professor in the education department. They have remained close friends, and Akers never has forgotten how Johns encouraged him to set goals and broaden his horizons.

"Seldom, if ever, do you exceed your own expectations," Akers says.

As a high school football, basketball, track, and tennis star, he expected a lot of himself, coaching Little League and junior high teams on the side as well as at the black school in segregated Blytheville. A 153-pound quarterback, running back, defensive back, and kicker at Arkansas, he continued to thrive on competition. As a senior he starred on the Razorback team which shared the 1959 Southwest Conference title with Texas and TCU.

By the time Akers was twenty-four he was head coach at Edinburg High School in Texas's Rio Grande Valley. Then he moved to Lubbock High School, where Royal hired him in 1966 on the recommendation, ironically, of Mike Campbell.

When he was named Texas's head coach, Akers asked Campbell to remain on the staff but Mike declined, feeling it would be an awkward situation, and ultimately took a job outside of football. Akers retained only two members of Royal's staff, recruiting coordinator Ken Dabbs and linebacker coach David McWilliams, then brought in other assistants quickly and went to work. He wasn't Royal's man, but in 1977 he was the right man at the right time for Earl and the Longhorns.

"Coach Akers motivated me," Earl said. "He taught me to deal with myself, to sit down and talk to Earl, to learn what makes me happy and do it."

Akers talked differently from Royal. He used terms like "comfort zone" (the level of performance that satisfies a player) and "self-talk" (crucial things a player tells himself). He stressed the importance of a player's having high expectations and not saying negative things to himself that register on his subconscious. "You can get good at being bad," he said.

Earl was nowhere close to getting that way, but he might have been close to getting fat. Their first personal meeting after Akers became head coach was in Frank Medina's training room, and Akers saw too much superstar to suit him. He asked Earl's weight and Earl told him 242.

"Well, I want you to lose twenty-three pounds," Akers said as he walked away.

"Where am I gonna find twenty-three pounds to lose?" Earl asked Medina.

"I don't know," the trainer told him. "It might be in your butt, but we are going to lose it."

Thus began Earl's pursuit of the Heisman Trophy.

Akers remembers an experience in 1974 when Earl was a 220-pound freshman and he was offensive backfield coach.

"I was curious about his speed," he said, "so one day I got up a race between Earl and some great sprinters we had on the team like Raymond Clayborn, Kelvin Scott, Gralyn Wyatt and Alfred Jackson. Ran them three times and Earl won every time."

He was changing the Longhorn offense, junking the famed Wishbone formation for something more varied. Earl would line up at left halfback in the Veer and at tailback in the I. Akers and his staff designed the offense to capitalize on his talent inside and outside and to use him as a receiver although he caught one pass his first three years at Texas. He saw Earl doing it all quite well if he slimmed down and speeded up.

When spring practice began in March, Earl became the priority project for Medina, the stubby, energetic Cherokee Indian who had trained Texas athletes for more than thirty years. Earl knew he was going to be put through the wringer. He had first met Medina early in his freshman year when he stepped into the training room where Medina was helping Roosevelt Leaks rehabilitate an injured knee.

"I heard him hollering and fussing at Rosie," Earl said. "When Rosie came out, I asked him who that was. 'Oh, that's Frank Medina,' Rosie told me. 'You'll have your chance to get to know him.'

"At that time I didn't understand, but later I would know."

Each morning Medina phoned Earl at 6:45, waking him up with a cheerful message: "I'm waiting on you." If Earl

tried to sleep a few more minutes, the phone rang again.
"I'm waiting on you!"

Earl always rolled out of bed and trudged to the training
room, trying to prepare himself for what was coming.

"I would put on a sweat suit and a rubber suit and get
in the steam room for twenty-five minutes," he said.
"Sometimes I would get hot and tired and crawl along
the floor to push the door open. Medina must have been
a genius because he always knew when I was going to
do that. He always pushed the door shut, saying, 'I told
you not to do that.'

"I got out of the steam room and did three hundred
sit-ups. Then Medina took me outside on the field and I
did stretching exercises. I warmed up my legs by running
sprints, and then he always had me run at least a mile.
Medina was always right there watching. He was one dedicated man."

When spring training ended, Earl had lost more than
twenty-three pounds. He was close to 215, but he didn't
feel good. He added a few pounds during the summer
while doing construction work in Austin, but watched his
eating carefully.

When he went home for a week, Ann Campbell knew
her son was dieting and she didn't fix him regular meals.
One morning she awoke and found a note on the dining
table:

> Mama,
> Wake me up when you fix breakfast. I *need* it.
> Earl

He reported for fall practice wearing a long-leg panty
girdle under his uniform, but that was to protect those
hamstrings from reinjury, not to hide ugly bulges. He
weighed 224 and was firm and fast. Akers and Earl were
pleased. So was Frank Medina.

"If a person doesn't have any goals in life," Fred Akers
says, "he's more apt to self-destruct than not. It's amazing

to see how many people never examine themselves and decide what they want out of life or football. It's mainly because they don't know how to talk about these things. They don't have a plan.

"That's where we coaches come in. We try to give our players a plan. It's a system they can adapt to themselves, because they're all different.

"But a guy like Earl is not hard to motivate. He's the kind of person who knows who he is, what he is and what he wants to do. He's not going to be sidetracked."

Indeed, Earl was all geared up and ready to go for his goals his senior year.

"They're very personal things that have a lot to do with life," he said. "They're not all numbers. Some are like never allowing yourself to have a bad day's practice. Never taking a lazy step. Like, I want to work at making a better fake on the pass play, or maybe a lineman has got to work harder on his pull. Things like that.

"I will not be denied. I will not be satisfied with just one man bringing me down, 'cause I know better.

"The thing is, he's got us working hard, harder than we ever thought we could be pushed. He's gotten us to keep on going, to keep on reaching."

And although Earl had no beef about his three years as a Wishbone fullback, he rejoiced when he learned Texas's new offense would consist of the Veer and I formations.

"It's what I ran in high school," he said. "It's nice to be back home."

Earl had been long since established as the leader off the field, a guy who got others out of bed and in the habit of making 8 A.M. classes as he did.

"It was funny to look out my office window about 7:45," says Rex Wier, assistant dean of the School of Communication, "and see Earl walking into the plaza of our building with eight or ten hulking players. He really pushed them."

Room 181 in Jester Center, Earl's room, became headquarters for friends seeking advice or just wanting to relax and rap.

"Earl," said Russell Erxleben, the super kicker, "is the father of the team."

"When Earl talks," says Alfred Jackson, the swift wide receiver, "everybody listens. I remember once a bunch of us were sitting around, just shooting the bull, and a couple of guys got into an argument. One guy picks up a chair and starts after the other one. Now Earl hasn't said much all evening, but when it looked like something was about to happen, he got up, went over to the dude with the chair, pinned him up against the wall, and said in a very soft voice, 'I think you better put that chair down . . . and sit in it.' That's all it took to calm things down."

Now twenty-two, Campbell seemed unusually mature not only to his teammates but to students who knew him around the campus. "In talking with him," says classmate Kim Brusenham, "you get the feeling you're talking with an older man who has paid attention to everything in life."

One thing Earl had paid attention to for years was the Heisman Trophy, which is awarded each December by the Downtown Athletic Club of New York to the outstanding college football player in the country, as selected by some twelve thousand members of the media. At the end of his discouraging junior season he was in the training room riding a bicycle when he heard that Tony Dorsett of Pittsburgh had won it. "Someday," he told himself.

Someday, of course, must be 1977, and Earl looked no better than a longshot in the early line. Other stars like Oklahoma State running back Terry Miller, Brigham Young quarterback Gifford Nielsen and University of Pittsburgh quarterback Matt Cavanaugh had enjoyed better seasons in '76 and seemed likely to be outstanding in '77. The UT sports information office did a low-profile job before the season opened. The cover of the press book pictured Akers and "Heisman Trophy Candidate Earl Campbell," an identification suggested by Akers.

There was no heavy pitch inside. Earl's credentials were listed in 14 lines.

In contrast, the Oklahoma State press book devoted the entire cover to Miller, and the prospectus referred to him as the "short-odds favorite in the 1977 Heisman Trophy race." Inside were nine photos of Miller, eight full pages of biographical data, statistics, quotes, and anecdotes.

The Longhorns never had produced a Heisman Trophy winner, and Akers firmly believed Campbell deserved to be the first one, but he felt there was no need for a blatant build-up.

"I'll push him, but that doesn't mean I'll go out and hire a blimp," Akers said. "I'm not going to buy advertising space or send out flyers, but I think it's my responsibility to help."

The candidate took a logical approach.

"The trophy doesn't only depend on Earl," he said. "It depends on the Texas Longhorns. If they're great, I'll be good."

And he believed the Longhorns might come closer to that than hardly anyone expected.

"We are in great position," he said. "I think this will be my most exciting year since my senior year in high school. You can tell by the attitude of the coaches. You can tell by the way your head coach dresses. He's sharp. He's got it together. The coaches are serious."

The Longhorns stampeded over Boston College, Virginia, and Rice in their first three games and got some attention across the country by outscoring their opponents, 184–15. Earl particularly enjoyed the Virginia game because he blocked on two touchdowns scored by younger brother Steve, who hadn't played in 1975 and 1976. But all of that was a tune-up for the Oklahoma game. When Texas won the big blast in Dallas, 13–6, everyone became serious about Texas as a national championship contender and Earl as the Heisman Trophy winner.

The Sooners ranked No. 2 nationally, Texas No. 5, and while it wasn't shocking that the Longhorns won for the first time since 1970, they did it in a pretty surprising way.

In the first quarter, starting quarterback Mark McBath was carried off with a broken ankle, lost for the season. Then No. 2 quarterback Jon Aune joined him with torn knee ligaments. Akers turned to Randy McEachern, who had done almost no playing in four years at Texas and in '76 had watched this game from the press box as a radio spotter. McEachern went in and played with amazing skill and poise. His self-talk must have been tremendous. That and having Earl in his backfield.

Earl had his finest hour against OU, breaking 24 yards for the deciding touchdown and gaining a total of 124 yards on twenty-three carries. And he was an inspiration on the sideline, slapping backs and rushing out to congratulate defenders as they came off the field after crucial plays.

Barry Switzer sought him out to shake hands after the game.

"I hope you win the Heisman Trophy," the Sooner coach told Earl, "and I think you should."

Earl was gaining momentum. Meanwhile, leading candidates like Nielsen and Cavanaugh had been sidelined for the season with injuries. Miller was having a good year, but Earl was having a better one, statistically and artistically, thanks to the surge of the surprising Longhorns.

But could Earl hold up for the entire year, with every defense pointing for him? Beating Oklahoma had been thrilling, but punishing.

"Sunday morning my body told me the Oklahoma game was the most physical game I'd ever been in in my life," he said. "I was still sore Monday night."

The Longhorns had no chance to relax after Oklahoma. The next Saturday they tangled with unbeaten, untied Arkansas in Fayetteville, and they had to score a touchdown in the last five minutes to win, 13–9. Earl rushed for 188 yards on thirty-four carries but he made the game's key play on a pass. It was second-and-ten on the Arkansas 29 when McEachern turned and threw to Earl in the left flat after a fake reverse. He evaded a tackler at the line and raced 28 yards to set up the TD.

By pushing his career rushing total to 3,385 yards, Earl set Southwest Conference and school records. On the Longhorns' flight to Austin he told his teammates on the plane's PA system, "I set a couple of records today, but

I want you guys to know that those records belong to you as much as they do to me."

He paused and added, "I'd like to thank Rick Ingraham for telling me which holes to run in."

Ingraham, a guard and one of Earl's closest friends on the squad, had perked him up when he fumbled after a 30-yard run deep into Arkansas territory in the fourth quarter. At the time Texas still trailed, 9–6.

"I had my head down, but Rick and the offensive line got me back up," Earl said. "They told me we weren't beat, that we'd get it back down there again, and I got my head up."

Shortly after that, he had hauled that pass 28 yards to set up the touchdown.

When second-ranked Texas returned to Dallas the next weekend and beat Southern Methodist 30–14, everything came up roses. No. 1 Michigan was upset by Minnesota, 16–0, allowing the Longhorns to take over the top ranking. And Earl enjoyed the most productive day of his college career, rushing for 213 yards on thirty-two carries.

"If they don't give him the Heisman Trophy," SMU coach Ron Meyer declared, "they ought to melt it down."

By now the media blitz was on, both in Austin and Tyler. Writers wanted the in-depth story of this tremendous runner who had charged to the front of the Heisman Trophy race, and they were fascinated by his family background.

Earl met them willingly almost daily as UT sports information director Jones Ramsey stayed busy hauling visiting press from the airport to the campus.

"Earl never stood me up on a press date," Ramsey said. "He talked to them from the basement of his heart. I must have had a thousand letters thanking me for all the cooperation."

No one got anything sensational, however. Shrugged one writer, "The most controversial thing he's ever said was 'nice block.'"

Earl did set the record straight on a quote attributed to him after he had six jerseys ripped off by frustrated SMU defenders while he raced for 213 yards. He supposedly said, "I just wanted to give them something to remember me by." But he didn't.

"When somebody tells you a phrase of me bragging or downing somebody," he explained, "that's not me talking. That's them."

Interviewers wanted to know about his social life. They uncovered no fast cars or fast women. Earl still had his girl back home, Reuna Smith.

He explained that on Saturday nights after games he went back to his room and visited with whomever dropped by. They might pick up some tacos, then watch television for a while. At eleven o'clock he'd turn on a black campus radio station and listen to a tape-recorded speech by the late Reverend Martin Luther King, Jr.

After giving all the details, he smiled. "Exciting, huh?"

One guy seeking to flesh out his story talked to a merchant on Guadalupe Street, the campus "drag." The merchant had extended credit to some Longhorn players and regretted it, but he found Earl was different. "Earl always paid on time," he said, "and even got some others to come in and pay."

Naturally, they always asked Earl how he felt about his chances of winning the Heisman.

"If it happens, it happens," he always replied.

At the old house back home in Jones Valley, Ann Campbell received as many interviewers as she could when she wasn't working in the fields or in someone else's home. She enjoyed the visits and they appreciated her candor, and her values.

Steve Pate of the *Dallas Morning News* asked how she felt about the prospect of Earl coming into big bucks when he signed a professional contract.

"What will I do if I get my hands on some of that money?" she mused. "The very first thing I'd do is pay off some debts I have. I'm not talking about a whole lot of money, but I just have to clear my conscience.

"There are some people I have borrowed from in tight spots, and I'd pay every one of them back. The most important thing to me is to clear the name of Ann Campbell."

During Texas's 26–0 victory over Texas Tech, while Earl ran for 116 yards on twenty-seven carries, Ann Campbell was introduced in the stands and the capacity crowd of more than seventy-seven thousand people gave her a standing ovation. Earl was kidded afterward about his mother being famous; but it was no joke to him.

"I don't think she could ever be as famous as I'd like for her to be," he said.

The Texas Tech game was the seventh of the season, and Akers revealed some interesting figures.

"We keep records on how tough the yardage is that our backs gain," he said, "and these are the statistics we really look at. Of Earl's 1,015 yards this season, 704 of them have come after first contact has been made. That's a pretty strong figure.

"A lot of backs go down when they're hit and only go as far as you block for them. If you block six yards for them, you get six yards out of them. That's not the case with Campbell."

Earl proved he also could break away from pain. The night before the University of Houston game in Rice Stadium, he developed tonsillitis and ran a fever. But he played the next afternoon after the team doctors certified him for action. You could never tell he wasn't feeling well— he bolted 173 yards on twenty-four carries, scored three touchdowns, and set up a fourth in a 35–21 victory.

"We were worried about Earl," Akers said. "He got tired in the pregame warmup and he was tired in the first quarter. I was afraid he wouldn't be able to finish the game. We kept cold towels on his head and made him as comfortable as possible.

Earl needed some time to shake off the effects of that day.

"I hurt," he said. "I'm like the old story of the man who itched so much he didn't know where to scratch. I hurt so much I don't know where to rub."

As Heisman voting time neared he didn't slow down. He blasted Baylor for 181 yards on thirty carries, and Texas ran its season record to 10–0. Then, before the showdown with Texas A&M at College Station, Akers told him in the locker room, "Earl, I really expect 170 yards out of you today."

"I'm ready," Earl replied.

He certainly was. He hit a new career high, rushing for 222 yards on twenty-seven carries, making three touchdowns and catching a 60-yard pass for a fourth. Texas won 57–28, to finish the regular season with a perfect record and clinch a Cotton Bowl date with Notre Dame on January 2.

Interestingly, the most spectacular performance came in the wake of a controversy over a racist sign at an Austin pep rally, a sign which Earl didn't see but heard about.

"I feel sorry for those kind of people in this world," he said. "I respect people and people respect me. I wouldn't know how to fight someone. We're all the same people, just different colors. But someday we're going to have to go to one another for what we want. We need to mix together and care for one another."

Thousands of fans were caring for the Longhorns, black and white, at Kyle Field that Saturday afternoon, Ann Campbell among them. But the rabid Aggie fans were too much for her.

"Nerve-wrackingest game I've ever been to," she said. "Those people stood up the whole game, for four hours. After a few minutes my legs just gave out and I had to sit down. I listened to it on the radio."

She gladly settled for simply hearing that her son was having the game of his life, and that he had won the national collegiate rushing championship for 1977 with 1,744 yards on 267 carries. He also scored nineteen touchdowns to lead the NCAA with 114 points.

The name of Earl Campbell couldn't have been stronger in the minds of Heisman Trophy voters.

HELLO, HEISMAN 8

THE DOWNTOWN ATHLETIC CLUB, which inaugurated the Heisman Trophy in 1935, broke from tradition in making its presentation for 1977. Always before the club had announced the winner, then honored him at a dinner in New York at a later date. This time it sold the television rights to the program, and kept the winner's identity a secret until the end of a fancy production which was aired in prime time on December 8.

This created a certain element of suspense in Texas. Everyone felt certain Earl Campbell would win and believed the rest of the country agreed, but they couldn't help wondering.

Earl was invited to the dinner, but so were a lot of other players. To create more awards to fill out the hour-long TV show, the club asked a total of eighteen players to come to New York—three in each of six different categories such as defensive lineman, linebacker, defensive back, offensive lineman, receiver and, of course, offensive back. One of each would be honored as the nation's best and, for the grand finale, someone in that number would receive the Heisman.

Earl certainly would have rooters in the crowd of fifteen hundred in the ballroom at the New York Hilton. Brad Shearer, the Longhorns' all-America defensive tackle, also had been invited, and guard Rick Ingraham paid his own airline fare to the Big Apple so he could use one of Earl's guest tickets and applaud his pal. University of Texas officials reserved ten tables for their party, which included administration and athletic department officials, influential backers, and special fans like Luis Murillo.

Murillo, who works for a convenience store chain in Austin, has attended Longhorn games and practices since 1952, and always gotten to know the players and coaches personally. Darrell Royal brought him to New York as his guest for what hopefully would be a unique moment in UT football history.

"In all the years I've been coming to the games and to the practice field," Murillo noted once, "only two people have ever invited me to join them socially. One is Darrell Royal. The other is Earl Campbell. They don't come any better."

To Earl's delight, his mother would be there. Ann Campbell was making the trip as the guest of two special Tyler friends, Mr. and Mrs. Henry Bell, in whose home she worked. She was pleased to be going, but staying in the New York Hilton wasn't nearly as important to her as her everyday life.

Just before Ann made the trip she was working in the home of Royce and Shirley Franklin, also old friends as well as employers, and Shirley suggested that her life was going to change as Earl became more famous and started making big money.

"I was just trying to let her know there were going to be a lot of demands on her time, that she probably was going to be more affluent and she'd have the opportunity to get around and do things she hadn't done before," Shirley Franklin explains, "If she didn't feel inclined to continue working for us one day a week we'd certainly understand.

"Mrs. Campbell drew herself upright and got a little

tcsty about it. 'I don't intend to change what I'm doing,' she told me. 'I like my life and I like my work.

" 'Have you seen the Citizens National Bank commercial on TV with Mr. Bell? He talks about the bank and how good it is and he says, "I know, because I work there."

" 'He's the president of that bank but he just says, 'I work there.' He can go out and do that because he feels proud about where he works. I do, too.

" 'I work here and I'm going to go on working here.' "

Earl was asked during the season how he would select the Heisman Trophy winner if he voted.

"I'd look for a guy who wasn't only a football player but a man, too," he said. "I'd look for a guy who was a great man off the field, and not just with his teammates but with people who aren't in football. I'd want a guy who knows people are looking at him to judge what kind of man he is, a guy who wants people to see him as a good example for kids.

"As a player, I'd want a guy who could do a lot of different things. If he's a runner, I'd want to see how tough he runs. A lot of guys can dodge one or two tacklers, but I'd like to see how tough he runs when he has to. Let's see if he can break tackles, not just dodge guys. Let's see how tough he is when it comes to breaking tackles when two or three guys hit him, too."

Earl wasn't trying to build his own case but his ideal candidate sounded a lot like him.

Back home, the rest of his family would watch the Heisman program on TV, convinced Earl would win. But that was nothing new to Willie Campbell, the oldest of the eleven children. When Dr. Earl Christian Kinzie had delivered his baby daughter during Earl's sophomore year, Willie had told him that Earl would win the Heisman as a senior.

Through his kid brother he realized the excitement he had missed in his own football career. Willie had been an outstanding center at segregated Emmett Scott High School in the '60s, but had never received any recognition outside his own neighborhood. He had had no opportunity for a college scholarship, so he had joined the Air Force after graduating from high school. Now he lived a few miles from Mama's house.

"I don't resent any of Earl's success," he said. "When I came along there were a lot of good football players here. We may have had some Heisman Trophy winners and nobody knew about them. But times change."

Herbert, the second oldest brother, experienced the same situation. He played tackle and, according to Royce Franklin, "was a tremendous athlete, maybe as good as Earl." Franklin, who coached at John Tyler High School when Earl and the twins played there, remembered watching Emmett Scott High against Texarkana and Herbert sacking the quarterback twenty-seven times. Herbert went one year to Jarvis Christian College, a small black school in East Texas, but left when a promised football program never developed. He later worked at a pipe and foundry company in Tyler and was badly burned on the job. He didn't enjoy a lot of breaks.

Royce Franklin says, "I told him once, 'Herbert, if you had been born just a few years later you probably could have been as famous as Earl and made as much money. Do you ever think about that?' 'Sure I do,' he said, 'but that's just how life is.' "

A few days before the Heisman program, Pat Truly of the *Fort Worth Star-Telegram* knocked on Willie's door, and Willie invited him in for dinner.

"Mama always taught us to open our door to *whoever* comes by," Willie told Truly. "She taught us all things are possible with God in your home. Oh, there have been bad times, but the good times made up for 'em."

Willie couldn't think of anything more fitting than for Mama to be in New York to share the Heisman glory.

"A woman who's done what she's done, worked for us, done things she didn't have to do, if anybody got to go it should be her. We're all proud of Earl. But Mama's the one."

The night before the Heisman dinner, UT president Dr. Lorene Rogers gave a press cocktail party and invited Ann

Campbell. Soon some of the Texas press were talking to her about the big event.

"What would be your impression tomorrow night if Earl doesn't win the Heisman?" she was asked.

Ann, looking her questioner in the eye, said, "Well, I'd just figure a more deserving player won it and I'll go congratulate him."

When the climactic moment came the next night, however, she heard her son's name called. Earl, wearing a yellow rose in the lapel of his tuxedo, walked happily to the podium, where he was presented the trophy by Jay Berwanger, who had won the original Heisman trophy in 1935 as a University of Chicago halfback, and O. J. Simpson, who had won it in 1968 as a University of Southern California running back.

When the applause died, Earl got a laugh from the audience with his opening remark.

"When I was a kid and got in trouble, I'd always say, 'Mom, I'm in trouble.' Well, Mom, I'm in trouble because I don't know what to say."

He really wasn't at a loss for words. He wanted to focus the attention of the crowd and the national television audience on his mother. Earl asked her to stand, and he grinned broadly as the spotlight found her in the crowd.

As usual, Earl spoke as one of the gang.

"The guys mainly responsible for me being here are my offensive line and all of my teammates. I will do everything in my power to represent the Heisman Trophy the way it should be represented."

In the audience Rick Ingraham glowed. That fall he and the rest of the line had made this moment their goal. When the offense wasn't moving, Ingraham would tell them, "C'mon, you guys, we gotta block so Earl can win the Heisman." And Earl remembered him as "the man who could always get me up when I was having trouble getting back to the huddle."

"Earl and I have been good friends since we were freshmen," Ingraham said. "We both like a pretty easygoing atmosphere, and we like to jack around together.

"The thing is, if you're not close to the people you're playing with, sometimes you'll have doubts in your mind about how they'll play.

"When I could see Earl getting tired, I just considered it part of my job to tell him that we were behind him and let's go. When he knows the line is behind him 100 percent, it gives him a lift."

The men who coached Earl were glowing, too.

"I'm happy for Earl," Royal said. "Things have worked out really well since he chose Texas. I'm happy for his family, and I'm happy for the University of Texas and the state, in that order. Heisman Trophy winners don't come along at our school every year, but neither does an Earl Campbell."

"I'm so proud for Earl and for his family and for our football team," Fred Akers said. "I know our offensive line is extremely proud. You don't see an Earl Campbell every day, and he is every bit as good a person as he is an athlete. He has a tremendous set of values. He has handled success very well."

After the program, photographers kept Earl busy posing with the trophy—a bronze figure of a runner, stiff-arm outstretched, on a black onyx base. It's thirteen-and-a-half inches high and weighs sixty pounds, but Earl carried it as easily as any football he ever cradled in his arm.

"I was too happy to cry and really too happy to even smile," he recalled of the moment he heard his name announced. "As far as I was concerned, winning the trophy was in doubt until a few minutes ago when I held it in my hands.

"I will do my best to bring honor to what the trophy stands for. But the more I think about it, I believe I deserved what I just got. This represents twenty-two years of hard work."

Earl was asked if the Heisman Trophy would change him.

"I don't think so," he said. "I've got two tests next week."

The photographers wanted Ann Campbell in a lot of

the pictures. As they stood in the big ballroom amid the flashing lights, the bad times and the hard times seemed far away.

"Mama, this is your award," he told her. "You've worked so hard. If it hadn't been for you, I wouldn't have gone as far as I did in life."

Back in Austin, there was a spontaneous celebration on the "drag" beside the campus when Earl was announced the winner. The UT Tower was bathed in orange light with a white "1" on four sides ten stories high. Celebrants painted "Earl" on car windshields and drove around honking, yelling and giving the "Hook 'Em Horns" sign with their index and little fingers raised.

Earl knew countless people were rejoicing with him that night, so he'd take the trophy back to Austin where they could see it. Then it would go home to Tyler to stay.

LOSING—AND WINNING

WHEN THE TEXAS FOOTBALL TEAM held its last practice on the campus December 30 and headed to make final Cotton Bowl preparations in Dallas, Tim and Steve Campbell hitched a ride with their big brother. Earl was truly a man of distinction—a Heisman Trophy winner who drove a 1967 Olds.

"Steve and me have a Skylark," Tim explained, "but that Olds runs better. Runs like Earl."

Three weeks had passed since that grand night in New York, and the glow lingered. The joy and excitement of Earl winning the Heisman was felt deep in the heart of Texas. But even in their happiness Longhorn fans still were annoyed by remarks Notre Dame tight end Ken MacAfee had made during the program.

When he had received the award as the country's outstanding offensive end, MacAfee had told the New York Hilton crowd of fifteen hundred and a national television audience that, while his team was ranked No. 5, it intended to vault all the way to No. 1 by beating top-ranked Texas in the Cotton Bowl Classic.

No one begrudged MacAfee and his teammates their ambition, but a lot of people felt he had chosen the wrong time and the wrong place to express it. It was said and noted, however, and ultimately MacAfee would be hailed as a prophet with honor.

About 4:30 on a bright winter afternoon in Dallas, whistling, whooping Notre Dame players rushed into their locker room. Before he went in the door MacAfee yelled, "The 'Horns were hooked!" It was January 2, 1978. The score: Notre Dame 38, Texas 10.

In the final voting the next day, the Fighting Irish, with an 11–1 record, climbed to No. 1 in the Associated Press and United Press International polls. Texas, also 11–1, dropped to No. 4 in the AP and No. 5 in the UPI rankings.

So it all worked out as MacAfee said and the Longhorns finished their otherwise perfect season in a bowl of Irish stew. Perhaps they shouldn't have been surprised. Nothing had gone normally during their preparation for the game.

Before they had even resumed practice, they had learned that their regular Dallas hotel, the Marriott, would not have room for them during Cotton Bowl week. The reason was simple: Notre Dame would be staying there.

A Notre Dame official, after an advance tour of hotels in the city, had asked the Marriott to lodge the team. The Marriott accepted, then told Texas of the conflict, in effect evicting a steady customer of the last several years. Naturally, this caused anger in Austin.

Marriott officials, embarrassed by the widespread publicity the foul-up received, offered the Longhorns free rooms at their inn on the far north side of town but were refused. The Longhorns instead took rooms at the LeBaron Hotel, not far from Texas Stadium in neighboring Irving, and it became their hotel for future trips as well.

The Longhorns also were stunned by tragedy. Fred Akers's brother and nephew had been killed in a flaming car crash at Blytheville, Ark., the day after Christmas. Akers bore up well, trying his best to prepare for what he hoped would be the perfect ending to his first season as Texas's head coach. But it wasn't to be.

Notre Dame coach Dan Devine brought his team to Dallas on December 22 and proceeded to praise the Longhorns so lavishly that some people were surprised to learn that Akers was allowing his players to drive to Big D in their own cars. They expected them to fly up from Austin without aid of an airplane.

"They're the best bowl team I've ever coached against either as an assistant or head coach," said Devine. "Though they're ranked No. 1 in the nation, I still think they're underrated.

"Texas may be one of the best football teams to come along the last ten or twenty years. The reason is they have no apparent weakness. Their Heisman Trophy winner is the fastest big back I've ever seen."

But on January 2, to the astonishment of an overflow Cotton Bowl crowd of 76,101 and a national TV audience, the wheels came off the Texas dream machine.

The Fighting Irish scored their first 31 points after grabbing fumbles and interceptions in Texas's end of the field. The Longhorns scored their only touchdown on Randy McEachern's 13-yard pass to Mike Lockett after time expired in the first half, an extra play made possible by Notre Dame pass interference on the previous play. That cut their deficit to 24–10, giving them false hope for the second half. McEachern never mounted a consistent passing attack in the face of a heavy rush, and was intercepted again the first time Texas had the football in the third quarter. Earl battled for yardage all afternoon, finishing with 116 yards on twenty-nine carries, but the game was as frustrating for him as his teammates. His running really didn't hurt a Notre Dame defense which was busy jumping on three fumbles and pulling down three interceptions when it wasn't swarming him.

"I felt we could throw if we established an inside running game," Akers recalls. "They had Earl in their sights all the time. When you can't go inside you have to do some things you don't want to do."

There were breakdowns in the blocking, and the defense, which found itself in poor position after all those turnovers, sorely missed middle linebacker Lance Taylor, the team's leading tackler. He was sitting this one out with a shoulder separation suffered in the Texas A&M game, and there was no adequate replacement.

"We just had a bad day," Akers said after the game. "You ever had a bad day? You saw ours. I'm always disappointed when we lose, but I'm more disappointed that we didn't show 'em our best football."

And Earl didn't show his best press relations at a time when it would have served him well. He was disappointed by the game and bothered by a bruised knee suffered in the third quarter, but that was no reason to dress quickly and hurry out of the locker room before he could be interviewed. All he offered were a few comments to a Cotton Bowl publicity official. It hardly was behavior befitting a Heisman Trophy winner.

"I am just proud to have been a part of this football team," he said as he slipped on his coat. "I wish it had ended differently, but it didn't, so there is no way to change that now. I could stay here and talk all day but I'm going to go now."

And he did, leaving behind his college career and a lot of unanswered questions. It was the only move he made all afternoon without someone in a Notre Dame jersey tackling him.

Earl had a far more meaningful conversation in Dallas when he had lunch with Mike Trope, the highly acclaimed agent from Los Angeles. Trope, although still in his twenties, had a reputation for making big deals for some of college football's most famous stars when they turned pro. The year before he had been instrumental in bringing Tony Dorsett, the Pitt halfback and Heisman Trophy winner, into a Dallas uniform, after Seattle traded its No. 2 spot in the NFL draft to the Cowboys for the fourteenth spot in the first round and three second-round choices.

Dorsett had been Trope's fourth Heisman Trophy client. Now Earl became his fifth. There was little doubt that Earl would command as large a contract as Dorsett had—a reported $1.2 million for five years. The question was, where would Earl wind up playing?

Tampa Bay, with the worst record in the NFL in 1977, would have the No. 1 choice when the draft was held in late April, but some much stronger, more attractive clubs no doubt would be interested in making a trade with the Buccaneers in order to draft Campbell. And Tampa Bay figured to be interested in a deal which would strengthen the team at other positions. John McKay, the head coach and general manager, had also had the NFL's No. 1 choice the previous year, and had selected running back Ricky Bell, whom he had once coached at the University of Southern California. The fact that Bell had also been a Trope client would possibly make the agent more interested in placing his newest prize with another club.

When they shook hands and Trope left to go to work, he knew his latest superstar was rather unusual.

"Earl wouldn't take an advance," said Trope, who frequently staked his clients to some cash until they signed a pro contract. "And he bought my lunch. He told me, 'Whatever money I have in my pocket may not be much, but it's Earl Campbell's money.' "

In Trope's early reckoning, Earl would wind up with the Dallas Cowboys, who had won the Super Bowl that season, the Los Angeles Rams, or the Oakland Raiders. The latter two were perennially strong playoff clubs and also in a position to bid heavily for Campbell's draft rights.

"Any of those three have so much material they can put together a package of players and draft choices for the trade without weakening their team," Trope said.

But by February 1, 1978, when he visited Tyler for Earl Campbell Day, the agent had revised his outlook. He told Carlton Stowers of the *Dallas Morning News* that he felt the Houston Oilers would figure strongly.

"I was on a plane with Bum Phillips after the Senior Bowl in Mobile," Trope related, "and he said for me to tell Tampa Bay no matter what offer any other team makes to come to him and he'd make a better one.

"I'd say at this point Houston has the inside track. If I

had to rank the contenders I would go in this order: one, Houston; two, Los Angeles; three, Dallas; four, Oakland."

What could Campbell do for each?

"He could put Houston in the position to be a contender. He could make Los Angeles into a Super Bowl team. He could make Dallas a dynasty. At Oakland he could gain 2,500 yards in a season."

Earl, as always, was inspiring big plans.

He already had inspired some in his hometown. No event other than the Rose Festival each October created the excitement Earl Campbell Day did.

A crowd of ten thousand people stood in a chilling drizzle to watch the downtown parade which launched his day. Earl sat on the back of a convertible with his girl friend, Reuna Smith, smiling and waving. He was deeply moved, knowing he was held in such high regard.

"People are always telling me that I put Tyler on the map," he told a banquet crowd of twelve hundred at Harvey Hall that night. "That's wrong. It was Tyler which put Earl Campbell on the map. You people took a guy and loved him and pushed him and made a kind of miracle out of him and didn't even know it."

The ashen taste of the Cotton Bowl loss to Notre Dame was gone now, washed away by the wonderful memories of so many special years. Fred Akers made it clear just how special.

"You're honoring a man this evening to whom generations to come will be comparing others," he said. "The things Earl did for us at Texas can't be measured in yards alone. He was a tremendous leader and inspiration.

"The only difference in the Earl Campbell I saw four years ago as a freshman and the Earl Campbell I know today is almost 5,000 yards and that trophy right there."

Akers pointed to the Heisman which Earl, true to his word, had brought home.

"In Earl Campbell," noted Darrell Royal, "I have a dear and sincere friend. His entire family means a great deal to me. When we were in New York for the Heisman presentation Ann Campbell said something to me which made me feel about as good as I ever felt.

"At dinner one evening she said, 'I've known you four years now. It's been a long time since you first visited in our home. I just want you to know I love you.'

"Tonight gives me the opportunity to tell Ann Campbell and her family that I love them, too."

Gifts for Earl included a Ford van from the citizens of Tyler, presented by mayor Bob Nall and Dr. Earl Kinzie, who had delivered the future Heisman Trophy winner and given him his name. Now Dr. Kinzie gave him something else.

He and his wife had put his old scales in a shadow box frame, and across the top he had written:

> First weigh-in scales of Earl Christian Campbell, March 29, 1955, 8 pounds, 2 ounces.
> Presented by Dr. Earl Christian Kinzie

It was a wonderful day and night, but Ann Campbell kept it in perspective.

"A few years ago, when my boys started making names for themselves as football players," she said, "I remember remarking that the Campbell family is a humble family. Since that time we've gone to New York, we've come home with the Heisman Trophy, and you people have honored us at this affair today. Let me say that we are still a humble family."

Then Earl returned to Austin and tried to settle down for the spring semester while awaiting Draft Day.

"After I leave here," he said, "football will become a business. Will that be less fun? No, because I love football. As long as your job is gonna be fun, you got it made."

STRIKING EARL

Dᴜʀɪɴɢ Bᴜᴍ Pʜɪʟʟɪᴘs's ᴇᴀʀʟʏ ʏᴇᴀʀs as head coach in the National Football League he knew his teams lacked an essential ingredient. The seasons were 1975, 1976, and 1977, a period which historians now refer to as Houston Oilers B.C.

Before Campbell.

Bum yearned for a running attack he could hang his cowboy hat on. He noticed Super Bowl teams always had one, usually built around an outstanding runner who carried a lot and occasionally far.

That first year, 1975, the Oilers had a surprisingly strong team. They won ten and lost four, but the game which loomed largest in Bum's memory was a 32–9 licking by the world champion Pittsburgh Steelers in a nationally televised Monday night game at the Astrodome.

"All I remember is Franco Harris having a great night," he said. "That might have been the night I made up my mind that I wanted a back like him. I wanted those other coaches to have to face that every week."

When it became obvious that some club could obtain the right to draft Earl Campbell in 1978 if it offered Tampa

Bay the right package in exchange for the No. 1 choice, Bum was determined the Oilers would give it their best shot. He asked John McKay, Tampa Bay's coach and general manager, not to accept any other deal without giving the Oilers the opportunity to beat it. He was certain a running back like Earl could become a tremendous strength for his team.

A lot of other clubs, of course, felt the same. Los Angeles, Dallas, and Oakland were mentioned often in speculation about Earl's future NFL address, and all of them were interested. Earl knew he would be moving into a championship cast with any of those clubs, but he admitted a fondness for Houston.

"If I had my pick," he said, "I'd want to play for the Oilers, because they're similar to what I like. They're down to earth, just good people."

That was nice, but the Oilers still had to offer Tampa Bay the right deal. If they couldn't, Bum knew he'd be watching Earl tear through a lot of defenses in another team's uniform.

Finally April came, and the time for decision was near. The twenty-eight NFL clubs would hold their draft of college seniors on May 2, and all eyes were on lowly Tampa Bay with that No. 1 choice.

McKay and his staff had evaluated a lot of players other clubs might offer and also noted each club's position in the drafting order. For example, Super Bowl champion Dallas would draft twenty-eighth, while Houston, with its 10–4 record, had the 17th spot. This had to be considered because the Buccaneers would take the other club's turn in the first round in exchange for the No. 1 pick.

The Cowboys, having engineered the blockbuster trade with Seattle that enabled them to draft Pittsburgh halfback Tony Dorsett just the year before, would have been delighted to put a powerful, talented runner like Campbell in the same backfield. Realistically, however, they weren't as inclined to go all-out on the deal as some other clubs were.

When the Cowboys first talked to McKay, he wanted a

quarterback in the deal. Dallas had none to trade and decided it didn't have a shot at Campbell.

No other clubs were willing to surrender a quarterback either, so McKay reviewed his priorities and then talked with clubs which still were serious bidders. He asked Houston for Billy (White Shoes) Johnson, the Oilers' ace kick returner and receiver. Bum said Johnson wasn't available, but told McKay he still wanted to talk with him again before he traded with another club.

By the third week in April, the Oilers and the rest of the NFL were hearing that Los Angeles was set to make a deal for Campbell's rights by sending Tampa Bay a tight end and some draft choices. One morning Jack Cherry, who was then the Oilers' public relations director, asked Bum what he thought McKay would do. Bum decided to phone McKay and ask.

To Bum's surprise, McKay was ready to deal with him. Even more surprisingly, he didn't want as much as Bum had expected. McKay said the Oilers could have the rights to Earl in exchange for second-year tight end Jimmy Giles, the Oilers' first- and second-round draft picks in 1978 and a third-round pick in 1979.

"I told him yes as quick as I could speak," Bum recalls. "He said he'd call his owner to get his approval and call me back the next day. Pat Peppler (assistant general manager) and Jack Cherry were in the office with me. When I hung up the phone, we just looked at each other, wondering if all this was a dream."

The next day, however, they thought maybe it was. No call from McKay. That was on Friday, and all weekend Bum waited and wondered. On Monday morning he got another shock. McKay had called on Friday, but since the lines in both Phillips's and Peppler's offices were busy, he had left word with the switchboard operator. Bum didn't get the message until Monday. Now he was worried that McKay might have decided the Oilers weren't interested and gone back to the Rams.

Bum called immediately, and was relieved to hear McKay say they had a deal—under one condition.

"I held my breath, wondering what he'd hit me with," Bum said, "but he just said he wanted our fifth-round choice in the next year's draft. I told him he had it, and the deal was teletyped to the league office."

It was eleven in the morning. Cherry called a one o'clock press conference, and the Oilers officially announced they had acquired the rights to Campbell.

The media also was surprised at the relative ease with which Houston landed such a tremendous talent and box-office attraction. Everyone was puzzled how Giles could become the cornerstone of this blockbuster trade.

Giles, six-foot-three and 230 pounds, had looked good as an Oiler rookie but not terrific. A third-round draft choice from Alcorn State, he was blessed with great physical ability and fine speed. He had good hands, ran with the football well, and had All-Pro potential if he could learn to block.

McKay, who had been hailed as one of college football's keenest minds when he coached the University of Southern California, had been hooted often his first two years at Tampa Bay, while his team won only two of twenty-eight games. This, however, had not shaken his philosophy of building the Buccaneers with gifted young players who could be the foundation of the club for the next eight or ten years. Because he stuck with it, Houston wound up with Campbell.

McKay wanted that package of draft choices, but could have gotten basically the same from Los Angeles. The Ram player in the deal, however, was five-year veteran tight end Charlie Young, who had once starred for McKay at USC. McKay and his staff studied both tight ends, and McKay preferred Giles because of his youth and potential.

"They did some homework on Giles," says Bum. "They knew what they were doing."

Giles did become a star for Tampa Bay, which improved enough to advance to the National Conference finals two years later. McKay must have been pleased with his choice. The Oilers certainly were.

Phillips, who is general manager as well as head coach,

didn't automatically pursue Campbell, despite his obvious talent.

"I wanted Earl, but I thought a long time about this," Bum says. "I had some misgivings. A lot of people have ability but not the work habits. Or they have the work habits but not the ability. This kid has both."

When the Campbell deal appeared set, Bum called Oiler owner Bud Adams, feeling an obligation to report to the man who signs the paychecks.

"I told Bud how much he'd cost us, both in terms of his own salary and other veterans who were negotiating new contracts," Bum says. "He asked me if I thought Earl was worth it.

"I said yes."

Earl was worth a fortune in season ticket sales immediately. Fans, seeing the trade as a really class act and commitment to excellence, swamped the ticket office with new business.

A Houston auto dealer was in Hawaii when he heard the news and quickly called the Oilers. Told all the lines to the ticket office were busy, he said, "I'll hold." And he did—for twenty minutes. When a salesperson finally answered, he was delighted to learn he still could buy a large bloc of season tickets.

Everything was clicking. The Oilers had just finished expanding their radio network from thirteen stations to eighty stations covering four states. When he was concluding arrangements with one new affiliate, Cherry had inquired, "Anything we can do for you?"

"Sure," said the new broadcast partner. "Get Earl Campbell."

That guy must have figured he never did business with a more accommodating bunch than the Houston Oilers.

It was a deal which impressed everyone. "You know the old cliche about the kind of player who comes around only once every five or ten years?" asked Bill Groman, an Oiler scout who played wide receiver for the club in its first three years, 1960–62. "Well, Earl Campbell is the kind that comes around once every twenty-five years. He's a better prospect than Tony Dorsett and Ricky Bell were last year."

Speaking from the offensive lineman's viewpoint, Oiler center Carl Mauck saw a lot to like in the Tyler Rose.

"The guy showed me how tough he was in the Cotton Bowl," Mauck said. "Notre Dame was a big, strong, rugged team. Texas didn't have any blocking and Notre Dame kept busting him up, but he got his 100 yards. He seems to be a helluva guy, too. In every interview I've heard him give he praises his coaches and gives credit to his teammates. He shows a lot of character."

Bum, keenly aware that the personality of a high-salaried rookie star can create squad harmony or kill it, checked on Earl the man.

"When you meet Earl," former Texas assistant Pat Patterson told him, "you're not going to believe anybody can be that honest and sincere. So you're going to be waiting for his true temperament to show through. But you can stop waiting; Earl is exactly what he seems to be, one of the nicest people you'll ever meet."

For a fleeting moment he also sounded like one of the most reasonable. Earl, interviewed by the *Tyler Morning Telegraph,* said that if it were up to him he'd "play for fifty dollars."

But agent Mike Trope worked on a higher scale when he negotiated with Oiler owner Adams and assistant general manager Peppler. A week remained before the draft, and Trope hoped to make it a productive one. He figured Houston should offer Earl an amount similar to what last year's top two draft choices Ricky Bell and Tony Dorsett had received, believed to be something like $1.2 million for five years.

"It stands to reason, and this is what I told Pat Peppler, that Earl is worth as much as they were," Trope said. "If Houston wants to make a deal based on last year's figures, without haggling over minor details, this thing will be easy.

"But if they come at me talking, say, 40 percent less just to bring my figure down, then maybe I'll ask twice what Tony got from the Cowboys. It's up to Houston to set the tempo. Personally, I like a rapid tempo. I'd like to get it settled by next week."

They didn't need that long.

Three days later the Oilers announced the deal was set. The contract was for five years and reportedly worth $1.38 million, although some of the payments were deferred for twenty years or longer. All that remained was for the Oilers formally to draft Earl Campbell.

May 2, 1978 was one of the longer days of Earl's life, and also one of the more memorable. At 5:15 A.M. the telephone rang in the darkness of his New York hotel room. Earl yawned, got up and dressed for his first stop—an appearance on NBC's "Today" show.

Next came a press conference after the Oilers opened the NFL draft by selecting him. Then it was time to hurry to the airport, only to find his flight to Houston had been cancelled. He waited awhile, caught another plane, and arrived at Houston Intercontinental Airport in late afternoon. Then he hopped a helicopter to the Oilers' practice field, where owner Bud Adams presented him the keys to a $17,000 baby-blue Lincoln Mark IV. (He returned the car two weeks later, deciding it was too expensive for his needs.)

Just up the street in the Oiler offices, the local media waited for his second press conference of the day. His mother was there, as were relatives and family friends. Earl felt at home, but he also felt awfully tired. His burnt orange blazer, so fresh when he had left his New York hotel that morning, was rumpled, and he had loosened his necktie. Someone asked if it had been a tough day.

"I'd rather play Oklahoma, I guess," sighed Earl.

He was not too weary to appreciate this moment, however.

"This is the realization of a twenty-year dream," he said. This meant he had enjoyed rare vision for a two-year-old, but after a day like this no one figured he had to have the numbers right.

In New York that morning Earl had said his goal was simply to be himself. "I'm not going to try to be Jimmy

Brown, O. J. Simpson, or Tony Dorsett," he declared. "I'm just Earl. It's up to Coach Phillips to rate me. The pace is much faster in the pros than in college, but I don't anticipate any problems.

"I want my teammates to accept me as a human being as well as a football player. In order for this to happen, I can't be nervous. Anyhow, if I get nervous, my blood pressure will just go up."

Now, in Houston, he was saying, "I'm looking forward to teeing it up with the Oilers this year. I hope I can be the football player people expect me to be, as well as the man."

The Oilers' excitement that Draft Day wasn't confined to Campbell. They had also traded their second-round choice to Tampa Bay, but in the third round they were pleasantly surprised that they could pick Brigham Young quarterback Gifford Nielsen. A six-foot-four-and-a-half, 205-pounder with a fine passing arm, Nielsen at the start of his senior season had been rated a stronger Heisman Trophy candidate than Earl, but a knee injury had finished his season after five games.

That knee had scared off many other NFL teams, but the Oilers were confident it was sound. Nielsen had showed no limp when offensive coordinator Kenny Shipp had gone to Utah a month earlier and worked him out. He had also scored highest of all quarterback prospects on an intelligence test administered by the Oilers' scouting combine.

As a junior Nielsen had thrown twenty-nine touchdown passes, and in only five games as a senior he had hit sixteen. His completion percentages as a sophomore, junior, and senior had been 61, 55, and 63. He seemed the ideal rookie quarterback to start grooming behind Dan Pastorini, who was entering his ninth pro season.

"He's got a good, strong arm and he's accurate," Shipp said. "He can find his receivers and he's schooled in the pro-style offense. If you had to throw the guy in, he could do the job."

In the fourth round Houston landed another Texan, wide receiver Mike Renfro of Fort Worth and TCU. His college team had lost forty of forty-four games in four years, but Renfro had played brilliantly and remained amazingly competitive in such a sad setting. A six-foot, 184-pounder with good speed and exceptional hands, Renfro at TCU had caught 162 passes for 2,039 yards, both Southwest Conference records.

Strange as it seemed now, the Oilers had been expected to draft defensive strength until they made the Campbell deal. Bum grinned when that was mentioned.

"Oh, we still did," he said. "Mike broke all the Southwest Conference receiving records and Earl broke all the rushing records, so it's been a good defensive draft.

"We ought to be able to keep the ball enough and score enough to keep the defense off the field."

Bum could afford to joke now. He had that runner those other coaches could worry about facing every week.

A BOOMER FOR BOOMTOWN 11

HOUSTON, HUGE AND HUMID, is a city of freeways. The nervous driver might want to pack two sack lunches for a trip from one side of town to the other.

Houston is famous for the space program which put men on the moon, for the surgeons who give people new hearts, and for the Eighth Wonder of the World, the Astrodome. Houston is a city of wealth—from oil, shipping, cattle, banking, and a myriad of other enterprises. And Houston is a city of tremendous growth. By the year 2000 it may well have passed New York and Los Angeles in population.

But cosmopolitan? Maybe so, maybe not.

"There are a lot of good folks in Houston," Don Meredith said once. "It's still a big ol' country town."

Houston is many things to many people, but in the summer of 1978 it proudly gained another distinction. Earl Campbell came to town to stay and play.

Earl was Houston's instant superstar, but he still faced some adjustments. Typically, he handled them smoothly.

He had a new jersey number. His number 20 from high

119

school and college now belonged to an Oiler veteran, defensive back Bill Currier. No big deal. Earl quietly changed to number 34.

He had a new home. Not one to seek the swinging singles life in a fancy apartment complex, Earl bought an eight-room house in southwest Houston and settled in. His cousin, Jewel Collins, helped him decorate and furnish it, and soon he was enjoying life in suburbia—watching television, listening to the soul music of Teddy Pendergast or the country-and-western sounds of Willie Nelson, Waylon Jennings, and Charlie Rich on his stereo, or shooting pool in his game room, a far cry from the dives where he had developed a professional touch with a cue stick during his Bad Earl days.

There were other famous names nearby; Oiler teammates Ken Burrough, Robert Brazile, Curley Culp, Dan Pastorini, and Elvin Bethea were neighbors, as were pro basketball stars Rudy Tomjanovich and Calvin Murphy of the Houston Rockets. But it wasn't celebrity status Earl was seeking. He just wanted to live comfortably and be neighborly.

"Sometimes we practically live off each other," said Adrian Burrough, wife of the star receiver. "Earl may come over and borrow a cup of flour, and we may go over and borrow a cup of sugar."

There were special touches displayed in Earl's house, like the shadow box containing the scales Dr. Earl Kinzie had used to weigh him at birth and the glass case holding a large cigar Oiler owner Bud Adams had presented him the day he signed his contract. And there was plenty of room for his family when any of them came to visit.

Ann Campbell spent some time with her son shortly after he moved into the house, but quickly realized Houston would never be the place for her.

"That town is just too big," she says. "I stayed a week with Earl, and in that week's time I was ready to come home."

Earl invited his older brother Herbert to live with him, but Herbert stayed home.

"Herbert is a country boy," says their mother. "He always liked the fields and raising pigs. Earl never cared for that. He was no farmer."

The fields Earl liked were the ones where he played football, and the Oilers certainly could accommodate him. First at the club's new training camp, at Angelo State University in hot, dry West Texas, then the regular practice field just down the street from the club offices in the Adams Petroleum Center, and finally on game days at their home in the Dome.

So there he was, ready to go, with a new number, a new home and a new kind of coach.

Oail Andrew Phillips has been called Bum most of his life, but that's fine with him. "It's a nickname," he says. "It ain't a description."

When he was a year old, his sister Edrina, who was three, began calling him "Bumble" because she couldn't say "Brother." In time it was shortened to "Bum," and today it's as much a part of him as his crewcut hair, wire-rimmed spectacles, Western clothes, and boots.

Bum is a native of the Texas Gulf Coast, so he feels right at home among the oil refineries, among the freighters steaming up and down the Houston Ship Channel, among folks who drive pickups and talk country in the big city. The only thing he liked about his three years as a Marine in World War II was the haircut, so he kept it. Conversely, he liked everything about coaching football, so he kept at it in high school, college, and the pros, enjoying a great reputation with his peers and tremendous rapport with his players for years and years before he finally got his big chance.

He was fifty-one years old before he became a head coach in the National Football League. It was 1975, and Houston had gone through coaches and general managers as frequently as it had losing seasons. Houston was the revolving door of the NFL, just spinning aimlessly, but Bum changed that. He led the Oilers to a different door, one which opened on a world of winning, competitiveness and camaraderie. The team wasn't blessed with an abundance of great players, but those players responded to their coach so well they became a force in the American Conference's rugged Central Division, which includes Cleveland, Cincinnati, and perennial power Pittsburgh, although they didn't have enough to make it to the playoffs and contend for the Super Bowl until Earl came along.

Earl also responds well to Phillips. "I enjoy every day I'm around him," Earl says. "He's so laid back. When he tells you to do something he does it in a way that you feel you don't have to if you don't want to."

Phillips motivates by osmosis. He enjoys football and wants to do well. His players enjoy his approach, have learned to appreciate the results, and they follow his lead.

He sets no goals. "If I got up every morning and tried to figure out what my goals were for that day," he said, "I wouldn't get anything done."

He has no guile. He's just a guy who loves what he's doing, likes people and hates double-talk. That has won him a lot of friends.

"I've been knowing him for many years," says Bear Bryant, who had Phillips as an assistant at Texas A&M in 1957 before he went back to Alabama and Bum chose to return to high school coaching in Texas. "I have never heard anyone say anything about Bum Phillips that wasn't complimentary. That's a pretty good testimonial, because coaches are an awfully jealous bunch of people."

"You have to coach your personality," Bum says. "I believe that's why a lot of guys who coached under Bear Bryant haven't made it on their own. They tried to be like him and they can't. Hell, there's only one Bear Bryant. He's a naturally dominant personality. You can't be that if it's not you."

So Bum's just Bum, and Earl relates to the way he handles things. "We don't have a lot of pep talks," Earl explains. "He just lays it out so that you know what you can do and what the other guy can do. I like his style. Let time change, but you don't have to."

Bum was immediately impressed with Earl's class in

training camp. Large crowds attended the workouts just to watch the mighty Campbell, but they simply saw another new man working to learn the system. Earl didn't show off or showboat against other raw rookies when he had ample opportunity to do so in controlled scrimmages. When the veterans reported a few days later, he remained low-key and humble—except for the day the older players yelled at him as he tried to ease out of the dining hall and demanded he climb up on a makeshift stage and sing. Then he was *off-key* and humble. But it was the spirit that counts, so they enjoyed his rendition of Willie Nelson's "Mamas, Don't Let Your Babies Grow Up To Be Cowboys."

"I'm an ordinary guy," Bum Phillips says. "Earl's not. He's a cut above that."

But to the guys who play for him, Bum Phillips is extraordinary. They like his casual manner and easy speech, but they respect him. One night during training camp Bum was running late for a team meeting, so he hitched a ride with quarterback Dan Pastorini—on the back of his motorcycle. They arrived in a roar, and everyone enjoyed the sight but no one thought less of the coach for it. Like Earl said, the man is laid back. The Oilers like it that way.

Most professional sports stars are eager to make extra money through lucrative endorsements, and Earl was no different from the rest.

"If I'm successful and people want me to do endorsements," he said, "I'd have no grudge against myself for running through airports" (as O. J. Simpson had done in a famous commercial).

By the time he reported to his first Oiler training camp, Earl already had a contract with a tobacco company to advertise and promote Skoal, which was sold more in Texas than anywhere in the U.S. The company had a number of other athletes on its roster, including former Dallas Cowboys fullback Walt Garrison and Boston Red Sox catcher Carlton Fisk, but Earl was the first black.

"I'm the only Skoal brother," he said.

The Skoal endorsement certainly added to his affluence, but he never flaunted his money. Acceptance by his teammates was most important to him; he wanted to be one of them, not above them.

"He doesn't talk very much," Bum noted that summer. "In practice he may say seven or eight words, but he's often singing a few bars of a song. Earl is shy, so it seems he would just as soon sit there and have nobody know who he is."

Earl has been influenced by his mother's calm, steady manner, and that was valuable to him when he had to deal with immediate stardom in the NFL.

"I learned to take things as they come," he said. "I'm really one of the happiest guys in the world. I just don't show my emotions that much."

His low-key personality was important to the chemistry of his new club. "Earl fit right in," Bum said. "He's one of the truly genuine people I've come across. He doesn't know the meaning of the word *I;* it's always *us* or *we.*"

Oiler fans didn't have to wait long for Earl to excite them with a spectacular game. At an August exhibition at Texas Stadium, he tore through the Dallas Cowboys for 151 yards, and his 55-yard touchdown run propelled the Oilers to a 27–13 victory.

"I didn't give Earl Campbell enough credit," said Cowboy safety Charlie Waters, a leader of the Dallas defense. "He's good, one of the best I've ever faced."

But not everyone in the elite NFL would accept that automatically. When the Oilers opened the regular-season schedule at Atlanta September 3, Falcon coach Leeman Bennett had to be convinced.

"I was hoping that if we got to Campbell early, he'd cough up the ball like a lot of young players do," Bennett said. "But we hit him and hit him and he never fumbled. He's going to be an exceptionally good NFL back."

In the Atlanta game Earl gained 137 yards on fifteen carries, including a 73-yard touchdown run with Pastorini's pitchout. That was the good news.

Any bad news? "Well," Bum said, "they beat us and I sure didn't expect that."

The 20–14 loss left some people wondering if the Oilers still weren't quite good enough, despite that rare rookie in their backfield. But those doubts subsided the next Sunday at Kansas City. Houston overcame a 17–6 deficit in the fourth quarter for a 20–17 victory, establishing a trend for rallying late and winning close which would become the team's trademark. That and Earl's big performances. Against the Chiefs he ran for 111 yards on twenty-two carries and scored both fourth-quarter touchdowns.

Earl became the third rookie in NFL history to begin his career with successive 100-yard games, joining Zollie Toth of the 1950 New York Giants and Alan Ameche of the 1955 Baltimore Colts in that exclusive fraternity.

Three weeks later he missed his first game as an Oiler, a 16–13 squeaker at Cleveland, with a pulled muscle, but rebounded quickly to gain 103 yards at Oakland and 105 against Buffalo in the Astrodome. Thus Earl had four 100-yard games in his first six NFL tests, and Oiler fans knew he was for real. They hoped the team, with a 4–3 record, was. And they would find out quickly, because the Pittsburgh Steelers, leading the AFC Central with a 7–0 record, were the Oilers' next opponent. They would play in Three Rivers Stadium, where the Steelers had rarely lost over the years.

The game was ABC's Monday night game, and other Oiler teams had stumbled around on Monday nights like the lights were off. Houston not only had lost all four games but had been outscored by a total of 125–33. But this was a different Oiler team with Earl, and maybe none of that mattered.

Earl didn't seem the least bit uptight about the trip to the Steel City. He just went about life as usual—and that included cleaning his house. So when Andy Bourgeois, the offensive backfield coach, invited Earl to join him and his sons on a Saturday afternoon outing at a small-town festival near Houston, he had to decline.

"I've got to mop the kitchen and bathroom, vacuum the carpet and take out the trash," he told Bourgeois. "But drop by when you get back and we'll have a Coke and ice cream."

When they arrived, Earl's place was spotless.

"It looked," said Bourgeois, "like a cleanup crew had been through."

Two days later, Earl cleaned up in Pittsburgh.

He cracked the AFC's top defense for 89 yards on twenty-one carries, three times blasting through Pittsburgh's proud goal-line defense for touchdowns. Houston won, 24–17, and Monday night football, with its huge national television audience, had a new star.

The Steelers, as physical as they were talented, were impressed by Earl's tough running style. After his third touchdown, a camera zoomed in on Jack Lambert, the All-Pro middle linebacker, obviously describing the force of Campbell's last carry to teammates on the sideline. For emphasis, Lambert punched a fist against the palm of his hand and then recoiled. Translation: this guy can hit!

"The Oilers," noted Steeler defensive end Dwight White, "are going places. I just wish they were in a different division."

The Oiler victory, so solid and aggressive, seemed a milestone to older stars like Pastorini and defensive end Elvin Bethea, players who had endured some miserable times during their Oiler careers.

"This kind of game has been a long time coming for both of us," said Pastorini. "Elvin has been here ten years, and I've been here eight. I've never had a more satisfying victory."

But the regular season was only half finished. There were more adventures ahead.

Incredibly, the Oilers overcame New England's 23-point lead to win, 26–23, in Foxboro, Massachusetts, and snap another seven-game winning streak. Earl ran into heavy resistance, but he managed 74 yards on twenty-four carries and scored a touchdown. Just before that game he had spoken of other priorities.

"I'm not concerned about gaining twelve thousand yards and things like that," he said. "My biggest goal this year was to play and stay healthy the whole season.

"I also wanted to come to the Oilers and mix in with the guys and be a friend. Not something fake, but something that was being myself."

The Oilers had been receptive and helped him learn the system, but he knew he still had some rough spots.

"I'm still working on catching the ball," he said, "and I'm trying to improve my blocking technique. I felt good about making a good fake against Cleveland and having the defense tackle me like I had the ball so Mike Barber could get in the clear" (for a 72-yard touchdown pass which launched Houston's 14–10 victory).

Then came a second Monday night game, this time against Miami in the Astrodome, and Earl was more dazzling than he had been against Pittsburgh four weeks earlier.

Late in the fourth quarter, the Oilers had the ball on their own 19, facing second-and-long. They led 28–23, and Earl had scored three touchdowns. He was breathing heavily in the huddle, but Pastorini wanted to get out of the hole. He called Pitch 28, which would send Earl outside right end—hopefully a long way downfield.

Earl was so tired he wasn't sure he could even get past the line of scrimmage, but Tim Wilson, the fullback, hit his man and Earl got outside to the sideline. "I decided to keep running," he said later, "until somebody knocked me down."

No one did. Somehow he found the energy to race 81 yards for his fourth touchdown, while the Astrodome's packed house sent up a deafening roar. When his teammates caught up with him in the end zone, Earl just smiled and sank into their arms. That was his twenty-eighth and final carry of the game, and it raised his total for the night to 199 yards. It also put him on top again among NFL rushers with 1,043 yards, making him the Oilers' first 1,000-yard runner since Hoyle Granger in 1967.

Earl, his chest heaving, his head bowed, sat on the bench

breathing into an oxygen mask when tackle Greg Sampson knelt before him.

"Helluva run, man," Sampson told him. "You won the game."

Sampson was right. Even though the Dolphins struck for another touchdown, the Oilers had enough to win 35–30.

Miami coach Don Shula was impressed with Earl from every angle. "He gave the Oilers what they had to have," Shula said. "He had some head-on collisions with our players, and I think he won them all. We had some people get run over that don't get run over."

The season was going full-blast now. The Oilers were 8–4. Everyone in town was raving about Earl, and how Houston could make the playoffs for the first time since 1967. It was a busy time, an exciting time and Earl made a basic discovery. He didn't have time to clean his house.

So he hired a maid one day a week to take care of it. But he still intended to continue doing the yard work; He had bought a power mower during the summer rather than pay one hundred fifty dollars per month to have his lawn mowed.

"Earl isn't going to waste any money," says Andy Bourgeois. "He's a most frugal young man."

The only place he splurged was the football field. And he continued his spree by rushing 122 yards on twenty-seven carries in a 17–10 win over Cincinnati, setting the stage for a second showdown with the Steelers. This time they played in the Astrodome, and Earl's mother was there to watch him. But the game ended early and painfully for Earl, who ran strongly in the first quarter but then was sidelined with a broken rib.

It was that kind of day. Casualties were heavy on both sides, but the Oilers got the worst of it while the Steelers had the best of the score, 13–3. Ann Campbell wasn't eager to return for another game, because she saw her son play only briefly before getting hurt.

"That kinda got off with me," she says. "I understand

you never know what is going to happen, but I really was looking forward to his performing through the whole game. He called me up there in the box and just said his ribs were bruised and he *might* go back in the game."

Broken rib not withstanding, Earl was back the following Sunday at New Orleans. So was Pastorini, who had suffered three broken ribs, and the Oilers earned a playoff spot with a 17–12 win. Then the team let down and suffered a 45–24 loss to San Diego in the final regular-season game at the Astrodome. But it was still a significant game for Earl. His 77 yards on fourteen carries gave him a regular-season total of 1,450 yards on 302 carries and the NFL rushing championship. He was the first rookie to win the title since Cleveland's Jim Brown in 1957.

He had had a tremendous season and Houston, 10–6 and proud to be in the playoffs, knew it was a better team because of him. But Earl knew he wouldn't have made it without a lot of help from his friends—particularly Conway Hayman, the seven-year veteran guard.

"I guess Conway was my strength," Earl said. "Lots of times I would just sit around with him at home, talking about the game. He'd tell me what to expect from his defensive man, and which way the line was going to block. He'd tell me, 'You don't have anything to be afraid of. That man over there is just like you are.'"

Earl took the message to heart, and took over.

That shellacking by San Diego made some people ask if the Oilers could be a factor in the playoffs, but the Miami Dolphins weren't among them. The memory of Earl's Monday night masterpiece was fresh and they knew they must stop him in order to win the battle of AFC wild-card qualifiers.

They came closer in the Orange Bowl on Christmas Eve, but the Oilers found another way to win, 17–9. Earl, with the Dolphin defense keying on him, gave a solid performance with 84 yards on twenty-six carries and scored a touchdown. Pastorini, wearing a brace on his injured right knee and a flak jacket to protect his ribs, passed masterfully, hitting twenty of twenty-nine for 306 yards and the other touchdown.

The Oilers were rolling, and the next stop was New England. Carl Mauck decided they should have a song to describe their momentum. So the Oiler center jotted down some lyrics, adapted them to the melody of "The Wabash Cannonball," made a quick recording, and soon Houston radio stations were playing "The Oiler Cannonball."

> From sunny Miami, Florida,
> To icy Boston, Mass.
> From the Broncos of Colorado
> To the iron in the Steelers' masks.
> He's mighty tough and rugged,
> He's feared quite well by all.
> He's the winning combination
> Of the Oiler Cannonball.
>
> Now listen to the blockin',
> The rambling and the roar,
> As he slides along the sidelines,
> By the hashmarks then the score.
> From the fancy-passin' Dago,
> To the Tyler bowling ball.
> Those Patriots can be taken,
> By the Oiler Cannonball.

The song was right. Houston had it all that frigid New Year's Eve in Schaefer Stadium and won easily, 31–14. The Patriot defense couldn't cope with the Oilers' weapons—Pastorini passed smartly, connecting on twelve of fifteen for 200 yards and three touchdowns, aided by Earl's constant threat on the ground. He gained 118 yards on twenty-seven carries, scored the other touchdown, and gave the offense a beautiful balance.

But all of this proved a big build-up for a terrible letdown. The AFC championship game, which determined the conference representative in Super Bowl XIII at Miami, was played in Pittsburgh, and Three Rivers Stadium that first Sunday in January was nothing like it had been that Monday night in October.

The game was played in freezing rain and the Oilers, despite their proud predictions of an all-out war, were never in it. They simply couldn't cope with the lousy conditions, but the Steelers thrived on them.

"It was a nasty day," said Dwight White after the 34–5 victory earned them a Super Bowl date with Dallas, "and nasty days are right up our alley."

The Oilers still had some hope as halftime neared and Pittsburgh led 14–3, but then in an incredible forty-eight-second span the Steelers converted three Oiler fumbles to 17 points and a 31–3 lead. Terry Bradshaw threw amazingly well in that mess, while Lynn Swann and John Stallworth caught the ball like it was dry.

"You gotta look it square in the eye," Bum Phillips said. "They had their best day. We didn't."

Bum took off his cowboy hat and shook ice flecks off the brim. The Steelers were so superior on this day he could even grin a little.

"The behinder we got," he said, "the worse it got."

The Oilers' game plan had been to establish ball control with Earl's running, then have Pastorini throw play-action passes. But they never kept the ball long enough to do anything. The Oilers lost four fumbles and Pastorini suffered five interceptions. Earl finished with 62 yards on twenty-two carries, but through three quarters he managed only 37 on nineteen against the swarming Steelers. And his fumble set up Pittsburgh's second touchdown from the Houston 17-yard line.

"You know, I've tried all my life to be a champion," Earl said, "but today it just wasn't meant to be.

"It was tough out there because your hands froze. You'd have the ball and all of a sudden it was just floating out there."

It wasn't his kind of track.

"Ice and wet fields hurt Earl because he doesn't run

straight up," Bum says. "When Earl turns a corner, his feet are out here and his shoulders are over there. He's leaning all the time. You knew damn well his feet were gonna go out from under him, which they did. It not only affects a man's running, but he's always afraid he's *gonna* slip."

The Pittsburgh weather continued to bother the Oilers after the game. Icy rain turned to heavy snow and delayed their takeoff from the airport three hours. Finally, they landed in Houston and felt foolish boarding buses to the Astrodome for a pep rally which had been scheduled and promoted by a local radio station before they went to Pittsburgh. They had lost badly and they were terribly late. Nobody would be there.

But when the buses headed through the centerfield gate and down the ramp toward the field, the players and coaches were astounded. There were forty-six thousand fans standing to salute them, yelling and waving blue-and-white pompons.

Then they realized that one lousy afternoon in Pittsburgh hadn't ruined a fine year for their fans, and it shouldn't for them either. It was something to cherish, to build on.

Suddenly everything was in perspective; they felt close to their fans and to each other.

Earl summed it up well.

"This isn't the end of the world," he said. "Just the end of the season."

THAT SPECIAL SPRING

PLAYER OF THE YEAR. Rookie of the Year. No. 1 rusher in the National Football League. Earl Campbell won so many honors he could have spent most of the off-season just traveling to banquets and programs to collect them. A tuxedo could have become his second uniform.

But he had other plans.

He wanted to slip on jeans and T-shirt and settle back into campus life at the University of Texas in Austin. Earl needed twelve semester hours to complete work on his degree in speech communication, and his goal was to graduate in the spring of 1979.

So he didn't appear at every function and personally accept his award. This upset some people. The Professional Football Writers of America, for example, wished to honor Earl as its Player of the Year in a pregame ceremony at the Super Bowl in Miami, and some members were disturbed when he didn't attend. Earl insisted he needed to stay in Austin, where he was completing registration for classes and renting an apartment for the spring semester before he left for the Pro Bowl in Los Angeles.

To him it was a matter of priorities. For the past six

months he had given himself to football. Now he wanted
to give some time to other interests.

"I'd like to apologize for not being able to attend every
banquet and golf tournament I was invited to," he said
later. "I had something I wanted to do at that particular
time that was making Earl Campbell happy. I couldn't lay
it down and say, 'Well, I'll go to school next year.'

"I really got a thrill from every award I won, but it just
so happened I couldn't pick up every one. You know how
life is. You're not on the same page every day."

The urge to return to school was no whim. "It's something I wanted to do long before I went into pro football,"
he said. "For years I had dreamed of earning my degree.
Now I wanted to go back and pick up my pieces."

This was an important part of his life. He would have
felt less a man if he hadn't done it. There was a limit to
how long football acclaim could fulfill him.

"Records," Earl mused once. "Somebody will always
break records. It is how you live that counts."

Academically, Earl was not outstanding, but he was determined. No one accused him of being a superjock expecting a free ride.

"Earl's a legend as a student," says Joe Eivens, academic
counselor for the UT athletic department. "You could
count on your fingers the classes he missed in four years.
That degree was very important to him. He studied very
hard and was very conscientious. Earl told me once, 'Mr.
Eivens, I learned a long time ago that life don't owe you
nothing.' "

In Tyler, work was underway to make another of Earl's
dreams a reality—that new house for his mother. This one
preceded his great urge to earn a college degree; it dated
back to hot summer nights when Ann Campbell and her
children found the sleeping cooler on the front porch than
in their crowded bedrooms.

"My goal in life," Earl had said in high school, "is to
build a house for my mother so that when she lies down
at night she can't see the Big Dipper."

His dedication to that goal, like his devotion to his mother, never faltered. Now the house was under construction, and would be finished by Easter—a lasting gift of love.

"People probably wonder why I talk about my mama so much," Earl said once. "One reason is that she's so great, and another one is that I believe if you are going to let anyone know how you feel about them, don't wait until they die. Always give them roses while they are alive, so they can smell them and see them."

Contractor Joe T. Coleman of Tyler agreed to build the house, and knew that Earl wanted his mother to have a place that was spacious, comfortable, and designed for family living.

"Earl said from the beginning that he wasn't interested in this house being a mansion or a showplace," Coleman notes. "He wanted something that was attractive and pleasing to his mother."

The design reflected Ann Campbell's wishes. "I want a real large family room where we can all gather," she said. "I want a real large patio where we can be." And she wanted her bedroom, the first private one she'd ever had, to be "kinda out away from the rest of the house, because Ronnie (her youngest, a high school junior) likes to play his hi-fi loud."

But as soon as they broke ground and the bulldozers leveled the site, there was a problem. Water was needed to settle the soil, and the Campbell well was dry.

Willie, Earl's oldest brother, hauled water in by hand for a couple of days, but it wasn't enough. The next night, however, a long, soaking rain began. "The Lord knows," Ann said.

While Earl couldn't appear everywhere to accept all of the twenty-nine awards his sensational rookie year brought him, he did make some of the banquets. In Dallas, the All Sports Association honored him with the Field Scovell Award, given annually for excellence in athletic vigor, integrity, and achievement. This occasion gave Earl an opportunity to visit with Bum Phillips, who was being honored by the Texas Sports Writers Association as the state's Professional Coach of the Year. Bum went formal, wearing a tuxedo with his cowboy boots.

In Austin, Governor Bill Clements designated Earl Campbell Day in Texas, and the big pink granite Capitol was filled with cheers when Earl, his family, and friends visited the packed Senate chamber.

Secretary of State George Strake, noting he was a native Houstonian who had sat through two 1–13 Oiler seasons in the pre-Campbell era, said, "This one man has united Houstonians and united Texans as never before."

Senator Peyton McKnight of Tyler was beaming. "It always is fitting and proper to pay tribute to a great athlete," McKnight said, "and it's even more fitting to pay tribute to a fine Christian gentleman who has evidenced his love for his family and God many times."

And the Rev. Gerald Mann, chaplain of the Texas Senate, offered one of Earl's favorite prayers: "I ain't what I ought to be, but I ain't what I used to be, and thank God, I ain't what I'm gonna be."

One day after class Earl dropped by the office of Rex Wier, the assistant dean in the School of Communication who had befriended and guided him since his first college days.

"What are you doing Friday and Saturday?" Earl asked him.

"Nothing special," Wier replied.

"Would you like to go to California with me?" Earl asked. "I'm going to receive an award on the Bob Hope Show they're taping in Burbank."

"Yes, Earl, I'd be glad to go," Wier said.

Earl smiled. "Good. I want you to go. I want my friends who were with me before I got all this money and fame to enjoy a little of it with me."

Earl thought his professor would enjoy seeing the NBC studio and how everyone operated during the taping of the Hope show. He also invited his brother Tim, recovering from knee surgery which had forced him to miss practically all of the previous UT football season. So on Friday they were seated in the first class section of a Houston-to-Los Angeles flight. A stewardess asked if she could take their meal orders.

"Earl told her that he and Tim didn't want anything," Wier said, "because they had brought hamburgers. There's a woman in Houston who makes hamburgers the way he likes them, and he had picked up a sackful just before our flight. To me, that was a wonderful thing. Earl was confident enough and comfortable enough to brown-bag it in first class without worrying how it would look to others."

Bob Hope presented Earl with the Great American Youth award as the professional male athlete of the year. Just before the taping began, Earl was handed his copy of the script. He studied it quickly, then stepped in front of the cameras.

"The first time Earl blew a line, Hope quipped something about it," Wier said. "They started over and Hope blew a line. Earl quipped right back at him. The audience ate it up."

The show went smoothly after that, and the next day they were jetting back to Texas. Earl's only regret was he didn't have another sack of hamburgers.

Then there was the day at John Tyler High School when Earl's jersey number, 20, was retired to highlight the dedication of the new gymnasium. It was more than a tribute to a great football career.

"We wanted to honor him for what he had done for human relations in this school and community," says principal C. C. Baker. There was a large turnout of family, friends, former teammates, and coaches, plus the school's student body and faculty. Earl was touched deeply. As tears streamed down his cheeks, he told the audience, "I want you to know that wherever I go I'm going to try to hold my head high. I'm going to give it my best punch.

"I really enjoy playing for the Houston Oilers. They're a great bunch of guys. I've really been fortunate over the years to be a part of great football teams. As long as I've been playing my teammates have put it on the line for me, and I really appreciate that.

"I'm sorry for my face being messy, but these are just happy tears, ladies and gentlemen. Thank you very much."

In Austin, Earl lived quietly. He shared an apartment with two old Longhorn temmates turned pro—wide receiver Alfred Jackson of the Atlanta Falcons and defensive back Raymond Clayborn of the New England Patriots. When he wasn't in class, he spent a lot of his time on the lake fishing.

He now had an agent in Austin, and Witt Stewart got plenty of action. There were a number of requests to have Earl endorse this or that, appear here or there. A great many charities also felt Earl would be ideal for their particular campaigns. With Stewart's help, Earl settled on two—Easter Seals and sickle cell anemia, which his sister Margaret has.

In Tyler, Joe T. Coleman told Ann Campbell the new house soon would be ready. Each day she looked out the window of the old house and watched the builders working on that new one. It was so near, yet so far. It was very much a family house, just as the old one had been, but it was very different.

There were central air-conditioning, carpeting, a fireplace for cold nights in the family room, overhead fans for warm nights on the patio, a formal living room, a dining room, a modern kitchen, four bedrooms, and three bathrooms. The antique brick, which Earl selected, had been reclaimed from an old East Texas bank building.

The house cost approximately $85,000 and it was Earl's gift to her. But one day each week she continued to clean the home of her old friends, Royce and Shirley Franklin, because it was what she enjoyed doing. "She can get away from all the commotion at home," Shirley Franklin explains. "She has time to do her work, watch TV, and relax. And our house always looks great when we come home."

In early April she began moving things from the old house to the new one, but she continued sleeping in the old one. New furniture arrived, including an entire dining room of furniture which was her fee from a Houston company for doing a TV commercial with Earl. Joe T. Coleman and his wife Mary had finished a handsome display corner for the Heisman Trophy in the living room. The house has 2,630 square feet of living area—three times the size of the old one—and four of her children would live with her. Her youngest, Ronnie and Margaret, each had a bedroom. Two older sons, Herbert and Alfred, shared another. On Easter Sunday she served a family dinner in the new house. Then the next night she slept in her new room the first time.

She was happy she was there but glad the old house wasn't gone.

"One time, when we first started building this house last winter, I wanted to tear it down," Ann Campbell recalls. "I said I'd had enough memories there. But time passed and I thought some more. I decided I really wasn't using good judgment there, because I was thinking about what people would say if we left it there.

"I decided it didn't matter what the public says. It's what you feel in your heart that counts."

So the old house with the tattered auto seat resting on the rickety front porch would stay. Oh, some of her sons planned to build a fence around it, and Mama wanted to have the roof patched so "it doesn't rain in the closet," but there would be no major redecoration.

"We're not going to do so much work on it that it will take away from it," she says. "We want it to look like it looks *now*. Earl plans to come back to Tyler to live some day. He said he might just put his trophies in it."

But not the Heisman. It has a permanent home in the new living room, in front of those floor-to-ceiling mirrors which give you four views of that memento of Earl's spectacular senior season with the Longhorns. That is Mama's trophy to keep, just like the new house is.

"It was kinda hard for me to move," she says. "I kept making my bed down there in that old house. It was just a funny feeling for me, leaving there after all those years.

But Earl had done this house for me, and it was time for me to move. When I went to bed my first night, though, I slept good. Now I'm enjoying it, I tell you for sure."

The house was tastefully decorated with touches of dark blue, orange, and light blue in various rooms as reminders of Earl's high school, college, and professional loyalties. In some rooms the furniture was shiny new, but in others were some refinished old pieces which Ann Campbell treasures. The family room is her pride. Aside from a giant-screen TV set which Earl gave her the first Mother's Day there, all the furniture is from the old house.

"That represents lots of years of living and working," she says. "I love that bench right there in front of the fireplace. Lots of my kids sat on that bench at the dinner table. I could get four on it when they were little. When I was growing up my parents always had a bench, and I always wanted one in my house. Now if some of the kids bring some friends home, we can pull it up and make plenty of room at our table.

"I'm kinda funny. I know the new-fangled things are nice, but whatever you have, if you worked hard for it, you love it and cherish it."

Old friends rejoiced for her when the new house was finished, knowing it would be filled with love and faith, just as the old one always had been. Pat Harris, whose husband Al was one of Earl's first coaches at Moore Junior High, told Ann that a number of women wanted to give her a shower for the new house. Ann was pleased, but was uncertain if she had the proper dress for the occasion.

"Anything you want to wear will be fine," Pat Harris told her. "This is for you. Wear the dress you feel is right for you."

Ann did that. She wore the dress she had worn on her wedding day almost thirty-seven years before.

Soon it was obvious that everyone who came to Tyler wanted to see the house Earl Campbell built for his mama. Jimmy Dean dropped by and brought Ann one hundred pounds of his sausage. And a lot of people came unexpectedly. Once she answered the doorbell and found a chartered bus loaded with curious visitors in the driveway.

Ann tried to be hospitable with everyone, but she could do just so much.

She had to tell one family which appeared unannounced that the house wasn't presentable that day. They persisted, saying they had driven a long way just to see it. Finally, Margaret called to her mother at the front door, "Mama, tell them to come back in an hour. I'll clean the house."

Instead of driving away and coming back at the appointed time, the delighted family sat in their car in the driveway for an hour, then rang the doorbell again.

Ann Campbell is a large woman troubled by arthritis, however, and the steady flow of visitors drained her energy. So an open house was held the first weekend in June and the public was invited to drop by and look around. Hopefully the pace would slow afterward and Ann could relax. The event was well-publicized, especially the fact that Earl would be on the patio signing autographs.

They came, all right. Joe T. Coleman, who organized the open house, estimates the visitors numbered between three and four thousand.

Old friends dropped by, too. Ann was delighted to see Royce and Shirley Franklin and their children, and urged them to stay after the open house ended. "We can visit then," she told them, "and I can show you something special."

When the crowd had left, she took them to the utility room behind the kitchen and pointed proudly to a new washer and dryer. Ann explained she bought them with money she earned at the Franklins' house.

"At last I can do all my clothes right here," she said. "For years I went to the laundromat. Before that we washed in a pot over an open fire in the yard. It's sure nice doing it this way."

Thus ended Earl's special spring. He earned his degree from the University of Texas, which he knew would please him and his family long after his football career had ended. And Mama had her new house, the product of loving, caring, and sharing. These were his greatest awards.

GIVING SOME MORE

THE AUGUST HEAT SCORCHED the practice field at Angelo State University. The players, their jerseys and pads soaked with sweat, pulled off their helmets and moved slowly toward the locker room in groups of two or three. All except Earl Campbell.

He brought up the rear, edging off the field a few feet at a time as he signed autographs for the kids who swarmed around, thrusting pens and scraps of paper at him. The odds seemed against his getting a shower before dark, for each time one youngster raced happily away with his signature two more joined the crowd.

But he kept signing and edging along until he reached the locker room door. Then he told the kids if they stuck around until he had his shower he'd oblige them. They waited.

Later that night he mentioned two special reasons he didn't want to disappoint the kids. Earl sat at a desk in a dormitory room in the modern high-rise where the Houston Oilers live during training camp. He wore typical camp attire: shorts, T-shirt, and tennis shoes. At this time of the summer, training grew terribly monotonous, but Earl seemed comfortable with it, accepting it as necessary conditioning for his second season in the National Football League. Just as he accepted those kids always waiting after practice.

"Some day when I marry and have a family, one of my kids may be waiting for one of their autographs," he said. "I'd like to think he'd stop and sign, no matter what the circumstances.

"When I was a kid I idolized Duane Thomas when he played for the Cowboys. If I could have gotten close to him I probably would have washed the man's car every day and toted his bags wherever he went if he'd just let me hang around. I was a nut for him. If I could be a running back like anybody I've seen, I'd choose his running style. Jim Brown was great and so is O. J., but Duane Thomas was unbelieveable.

"So I remember how I was as a kid, wanting to be close to people I saw on TV. I know how these kids are with Earl Campbell.

"It's a short life. I'd like to think every time I sign an autograph I make someone happy."

The consistency of Earl's personality certainly makes his coach happy. "For a year it was hard to believe a guy could be that perfect all the time," Bum Phillips said. "When camp started this summer I told him, 'You know, I don't think you *are* going to change.' He said, 'Coach, I can't. I don't know how.' "

Bum was sitting in the first-floor dormitory suite where he lives during camp. Practice was finished for another day, and he propped his feet on a table while he talked about his unusual superstar.

"What makes Earl different," he said, "is that he truly believes that the team made him.

"Look at all the honors he has won. I don't think he looks at an honor like it was given to him. He looks at it like the team won the trophy but he's the guy who accepted the award.

"I think down deep he doesn't accept any praise for

himself. He truly *believes* the team is number one. Now a lot of people *say* that, but they don't believe it. Earl's actions say it. He doesn't talk about it. He may go a whole practice without saying ten words."

Bum Phillips runs a comfortable camp. Sure, the workouts can get tough in that West Texas heat, and there are plenty of meetings, but a team can't become a Super Bowl contender by just dreaming about it. The players respect him, but they don't fear him.

Bum keeps some horses on a friend's ranch near San Angelo, and he's out there riding when he has free time. If some players want to join him, fine. He keeps a pot of gumbo on the stove as well as beer in the refrigerator, and staff members know they can joke with him.

For instance, Pat Peppler, the assistant general manager, has a lot of bare scalp where his hair once was. One day he put on a hairpiece, so changing his appearance that assistant public relations director Bob Hyde took him to meet Bum.

"Coach, this is Jimmy Johnson from the Baylor staff," Hyde told him. "He just came out to visit us for a few days."

Bum shook hands and started making friendly conversation, never realizing it was Peppler until the others started laughing.

Earl and Bum understand each other. One day Earl was visiting with his coach when an injured player came by, needing to talk. Earl stepped into the bedroom and closed the door to give them some privacy. When the player left, Earl couldn't get out—the lock was jammed.

Bum sent for a maintenance man who spent the next hour taking the door off by its hinges. Meanwhile, his star runner did what he knew his coach would want him to do. He lay back and turned on the stereo.

When they got the door off Earl was sleeping. Bum shrugged—a guy's gotta relax, you know.

"I've had three dreams fulfilled," Earl said that night in training camp.

"I always had a dream of doing things for my mother. I guess the house was the main thing, and now she has it.

"Another was going to college when so many people around me were telling me I couldn't. Now I've graduated.

"The other was playing professional football and being a successful man in life."

Being successful, to Earl, involves other people's help, so he wasn't pleased when Tom Fears, a former pro coach who operates a talent-rating service, observed that most Oiler players were average but looked better "because Campbell is so good." He rated Earl a "gold nugget" and gave him a perfect rating of nine. Fears said the Oilers had only three other gold nuggets—quarterback Dan Pastorini, wide receiver Ken Burrough, and linebacker Robert Brazile. He said Pittsburgh, which had beaten Houston 34–5 in the freezing AFC finals the previous January, had nineteen gold nuggets. It was like matching Olive Oyl with Raquel Welch.

"He doesn't have to be around these guys (Oiler teammates) like I do," Earl said of Fears and his ratings. "At two-thirty on Sunday afternoon he doesn't have to rely on them on fourth-and-one and see them make a hole for you big as daylight.

"Let those people I play with decide they don't want to do nothing on Sunday, and you'll have a chance to see what a gold nugget I am."

The next evening came the highlight of Oiler training camp, the barbecue at Hoolihan Acres, a tree-shaded recreational and camping site far out in the country along the highway to Fort Stockton. Hundreds of San Angelo folks drove twenty-five miles to toast the players and coaches at a party given by KCTV, the local television station. There was a country-and-western band playing and composer Alex Harvey, a pal of Bum's, sang some of his songs—such as *Reuben James* and *Delta Dawn*. It was a relaxed evening, and the Oilers enjoyed getting away from the cafeteria food and dormitory living for a few hours.

While Harvey sang and Bum sat on the side of the stage,

Pastorini stood in the crowd wearing jeans and a black T-shirt emblazoned with "Harley Davidson" in silver. Black and silver are the Oakland Raiders' colors, but somehow one wouldn't expect to see a shirt like that one in Oiler blue. The quarterback, a guy who enjoyed living hard and fast, seemed the antithesis of Earl, but he had always admired his young teammate greatly.

"There's an old saying about friends," Pastorini said. "Some walk out while others walk in. Earl's a walker-inner. Whatever you need, you can count on him."

Carl Mauck, the eleven-year veteran center, had just growled his musical creation, "Oiler Cannonball," into the microphone. Offstage, he sang Earl's praises.

"Earl's a tremendous human being," Mauck said. "When he signed with the Oilers he said he wanted to do three things: He wanted to fit in with the team. He wanted to build his mother a house. And he wanted to help us win. He's one of the real greats."

When the party ended, the Oilers headed for town to find more fun. "C'mon, Alex!" Bum yelled. "I've got your git-tar!"

One young lady kept looking through the crowd, hoping to meet Campbell.

"I'm sorry," an Oiler official told her. "Earl left early."

It figured. Earl enjoys a social but he also likes his rest.

It was a good camp for Earl. Physically and mentally, he was primed for another big year, seemingly not the least worried that he might become a victim of the sophomore jinx which causes some professional stars to stumble after a great rookie year. He was confident, but not cocky, when he discussed the new season with Hal Lundgren of the Houston Chronicle.

"I've never been high on drugs," he said. "I'm always high on life. I'm very, very high on my job, football."

Earl felt he was a step faster than he had been in the previous season. During the summer he had worked out in Houston under the supervision of Tom Williams, a former Oiler assistant general manager and Grambling College track coach who helped a number of athletes with their conditioning. Williams told them to run up and down the banks of the bayou behind his barbecue restaurant. His training was credited by Oiler receivers Billy (White Shoes) Johnson and Mike Renfro with speeding their recovery from knee surgery. With a big guy like Earl, Williams felt this would help to get his muscles loose to run with the football again.

After rushing for 1,450 yards as a rookie, what was his goal in '79?

"I don't have any numbers in the back of my head," Campbell said. "But I'm expecting a lot from this guy Earl. I understand him better than anybody else in the world, and he wants to do well. There's no way you can accomplish too much in life."

When the team returned to Houston from San Angelo, however, Earl could have been excused for wondering if there was such a thing as too much fan mail. He hired Oiler secretary Janice Boone on the side to help him handle it.

A three-week backlog resulted in his sending, at his expense, 987 autographed pictures. At twenty-two cents each, that's $217.74. "Earl wants every letter answered," Janice Boone said, "and he signs them all himself."

When he did, he wondered if someday he might have a child waiting just as anxiously for a reply from a superstar, as those children writing to him.

During Earl's college years, those serving Sunday lunch in the athletes' dining hall at the University of Texas would leave the pork chops and dressing and fried chicken on the steam tables because the Campbell brothers were in church.

"Whenever Earl and the twins get here," the supervisor would say, "that's when we shut down the line."

The lessons of their childhood had stayed with them. As Earl would note, "Mama always said, 'If you want to be somewhere safe, be in church.'"

He felt no differently after he moved to Houston. Earl began attending Antioch Baptist, a historic downtown church where his cousin Jewel Collins is a member. Antioch, the oldest black Baptist church in Houston, was founded in 1866. Its stately stone building sits on a wedge of land on Robin Street, surrounded by gleaming new skyscrapers. In the sanctuary, the sunlight filters through stained-glass windows and casts a pale glow on the dark oak benches where generations have worshiped.

He was pleased when the Rev. John Westbrook moved there from Tyler's True Vine Baptist as pastor. "If they called you as preacher," Earl told Westbrook, "I think I'll hook up here."

Earl had been a freshman at Texas when he first met Westbrook, the former Baylor running back who in September 1966 had become the first black to play in the Southwest Conference. Later, when Westbrook had conducted a revival at the Campbells' church in Tyler, Hopewell Baptist No. 1, he had come to know Earl better and also had met his mother, brothers, and sisters. Although Westbrook was minister of another Tyler church, he had come to know Earl well as the years passed. So Earl felt especially comfortable when he became a member of Antioch Baptist before the 1979 football season.

During the fall he had to miss a lot of Sunday services because of games, but he faithfully attended a Bible study group which Westbrook taught each Wednesday night. He missed it only once all season, when the Oilers were in Dallas the night before their Thanksgiving game with the Cowboys.

"That tells me something," Westbrook says. "He really wants to know more about God's Word."

"I go," Earl says, "because I think I need the strength.

"We've been studying the book of St. John, about how Jesus packed mud over a blind guy's eyes, told him to wash his face, and made him see. If The Man has enough power to make a universe, wake you up every morning and look after you, I just think it's nice to stop and try to get to know who he is and thank him.

"If there's a sinner in the world, it's me. I just go and try to wash [the sins] away."

"Earl has a strong commitment," Westbrook says. "His faith is real.

"I have worked with a lot of athletes who are Christians. I have worked with a lot who are nominal Christians. They would help us out because it was for the FCA (Fellowship of Christian Athletes). They would give a little talk, do things for kids, and sign autographs but there was no real strong commitment.

"Earl is a lot more serious about his commitment, a lot more than most people realize. He's trying to keep that commitment and I think it's a little rugged to do it, being a superstar with so many pressures. He can hold his own with anybody, though.

"Earl's Bible does not collect any dust."

The 1979 season began in a big sweat at Washington's RFK Stadium. When Earl blasted the final three yards for the touchdown which gave the Oilers a 29–27 victory, he lay face down in the end zone for a minute.

"How hot was it out there?" he inquired in the locker room, "165?"

Close. Actually the temperature was ninety degrees and the humidity eighty-five. "Earl ran thirty-two times for 166 yards in an oven," Bum Phillips said. "That separates the good ones from the average ones."

The Oilers won in their 1978 fashion, overcoming a 14-point deficit in the final eleven minutes. The bus ride to the airport was a happy time.

A lot of the Oilers wear jeans, Western shirts, and cowboy hats on trips—a distinct contrast to the Dallas Cowboys in their three-piece suits and neckties—but Washington was so steamy that afternoon before Labor Day that dress was even more casual. Billy (White Shoes) Johnson wore a lightweight jogging suit, the zipper of the jacket pulled down just above his navel for better ventilation, and stood in the stepwell by the driver while he recreated his biggest play. It had been vintage White Shoes—catching a short pass on fourth-and-twenty, stopping, turning one hundred eighty degrees and racing 29 yards to keep a scoring drive alive.

"It felt good to be out there doing that sort of thing again," said Johnson, who had missed the entire '78 season after knee surgery. "This is a good bunch of guys. I'm glad to be back."

Earl, soul music playing on the portable stereo in his lap, sat on the front seat beside Leon Gray, the newly-acquired All-Pro tackle from New England who was anxious to catch a plane to Boston to visit his wife and newborn child. When the bus neared the terminal, the driver started to pull through a side gate and deliver the Oilers to their chartered plane parked on the apron. "Hey, bussie, take this man around front first," Earl said. "Our plane won't leave without us."

There he went again, winning friends and influencing linemen.

But the next Sunday in Three Rivers Stadium there was no winning the game or influencing Pittsburgh Steelers. The Oilers never got out of the hole against the defending Super Bowl champions and took a 38–7 licking. And in contrast to the wet, freezing AFC title game the previous January it was a bluebird day, proving that when the Steelers are hot they're hot in any kind of weather.

Earl gained only 38 yards on sixteen carries, and as the Oilers fell behind they had to throw more than usual. To make it worse, Johnson suffered another knee injury and was lost for another season. When the game finally ended, the Oilers walked slowly past a large group of somber press people waiting outside their locker room.

"Smile," Earl said. "Or did someone die?"

The Oilers hadn't, but that game signaled the beginning of an erratic period for them. Pastorini, his arm weakened by a viral infection which deadened a nerve in his shoulder during the off-season, was passing poorly, and the team had suffered a long series of major injuries. Still, the Oilers won four of their first six games and were staying close to Pittsburgh in the AFC Central race. Then they went to Baltimore, and a different problem troubled them.

This time it was personal rather than physical. Pastorini and tight end Mike Barber, once close friends, were at odds and Barber had complained to the media about how few passes Pastorini was throwing him. The problem erupted in Houston a few days before they played the Colts and everyone was tense on the flight to Baltimore.

But at a Saturday night team meeting both players tearfully apologized for the disruption. The Oilers relaxed and beat the Colts 28–16 the next afternoon.

Pastorini's passing still was off, five completions for 49 yards and two interceptions, and none of the three he threw toward Barber connected. But both men claimed they had settled their differences and the important thing was winning.

Earl was touched by the reconciliation.

"I feel like they took a load of steel off me," he said. He celebrated by gaining 149 yards on twenty-two carries, his fourth 100-yard game in seven weeks, but he suffered a bruised thigh and was almost useless in the next game at Seattle.

Earl gained only four yards on three carries and the Oilers lost big again, 34–14. He played the entire game against the New York Jets in the Astrodome a week later but carried for only 37 yards on eleven tries before the Oilers finally won in overtime, 27–24. Then the old Earl returned and ripped for seven straight 100-yard games, ranging from 107 against Oakland to 195 against Dallas. The Oilers, with the driveshaft of their machine strong again, drove toward the playoffs.

Again they could say thanks to Byron Donzis. Inventor of the flak jacket which had protected Pastorini's injured ribs in the 1978 stretch run, Donzis built a fiberglass pad for Earl's thigh. He added smaller, hinged pads to the larger pad to completely cover the bruised area of the leg, which previously had been left exposed between the kneepad and the conventional thigh pad.

"It saved the season for me," Earl says of Donzis's invention. "I took a couple of licks on my thigh, and if it wasn't for that pad, I wouldn't be playing."

When he hit his peak against Dallas in Texas Stadium on Thanksgiving Day, Earl had a large family cheering section in the stands. But his mother wasn't there.

"I'll be at home, having my dinner and watching the game on television," Ann Campbell had said before the game. "Earl and I have an understanding. He gave me this set with a big screen, and I can see the games fine right here. No sense in my getting out in those crowds with my arthritis, trying to sit on half a seat with folks jumping all around me."

Ann must have really been pleased she was at home to watch the emotional Monday night game with Pittsburgh December 10. The Astrodome was packed with screaming fans waving "Luv Ya Blue" signs, and the Oilers responded with a splendid performance for a 20–17 victory. Chuck Noll was impressed.

"I think the Houston Oilers played the best game I've ever seen them play," said the Steelers' coach.

Earl had a dandy one. His 109 yards on thirty-three carries marked his first time to rush for 100 yards against Pittsburgh. In fact, it was the first time in two years the Steel Curtain had yielded 100 yards to any runner. To cap the evening, Earl threw the key block for Rob Carpenter's 4-yard touchdown run, which provided the winning margin late in the game.

The Oilers were grooving now and so was Earl. He was leading the NFL in rushing again, and recently had received a rare honor in Austin. Before the Texas-Baylor game Earl and Darrell Royal had stood together on the field of Memorial Stadium, giving the "Hook 'Em" sign to the crowd after Earl's jersey number 20 had been retired. It was the first time in Longhorn football history that a number had been retired.

As UT-Austin president Dr. Peter Flawn said, "Earl Campbell brought honor to the university on and off the field."

Earl was also bringing honor to his new home city, and Houston responded enthusiastically. As a rookie, Earl had taken his offensive linemen to dinner at a Japanese restaurant, but Earl hadn't been allowed to pay the check. A stranger in the restaurant, an appreciative Oiler fan, had insisted on paying. This second season, Earl took them to one of his favorite places, Angelo's Fisherman's Wharf, and decided to invite a lot of other offensive players, swelling the party to around twenty. Earl urged his friend Charley Angelo to lay on a feast and Angelo, to the players' delight, did. When they finally had their fill and it was time to pay the bill, another big Oiler fan sent word to Earl that he wanted to pay it. Earl's teammates razzed him about inviting them to dinners he never paid for, but the fan insisted. The bill was more than a thousand dollars, and the fan left a four-hundred-dollar tip.

During the 1979 season a Houston meat company announced it would award each starting lineman twenty pounds of beef for each game Campbell rushed more than a hundred yards. Earl did it eleven times, an NFL record, and each of his pals took home 220 pounds of beef.

"That's a helluva deal," Carl Mauck told him. "Can you work out anything to get us gasoline?"

Earl wasn't through. When he wrapped up the NFL rushing title against Philadelphia and was honored as Player of the Game, he suggested on the Oiler Radio Network that the sponsor of the award, a large jewelry company, also give watches to the offensive linemen. The jeweler agreed, and soon each regular lineman had still another reminder of Earl's appreciation.

As the regular season ended and the Oilers prepared for the playoffs, Bum Phillips complained to NFL headquarters in New York about how Pittsburgh and Philadelphia tacklers had roughed up Earl when he was out of bounds. Other Oilers also were upset about it, but Earl refused to beef.

"Earl's the most unprotected back in the league," said assistant general manager Pat Peppler.

"I think because Earl is so durable the officials take him for granted," said guard Conway Hayman. "They think he's not hurt by that sort of thing. Also, Earl never complains. He's just not that way."

Would complaining help?

"If Earl did," said Hayman, "it would change things around."

But it wasn't Earl's style. Instead, he preferred to rejoice in the team's success and his second NFL rushing title.

He clinched that in the first half against the Eagles, exploding for 134 yards on sixteen carries, and then watched the second half from the sideline as Philadelphia won, 26–20. Since the Steelers had beaten Buffalo 28–0 earlier in the afternoon to qualify as the AFC Central champion, the Oilers knew they couldn't improve their playoff position. So Bum rested a lot of regulars in the second half and didn't fret that the loss left Houston with an 11–5 record, a game behind Pittsburgh.

The big celebration in the Astrodome that December afternoon was for Earl, who finished the regular schedule with 1,697 yards on 368 carries for a 4.7 average. (Chicago's illustrious Walter Payton ranked second in the NFL with 1,610 on 369, a 4.4 average.)

When the final gun sounded, the fans stood and saluted Earl for giving them another year to cheer about. He walked off the field between two large linemen, Leon Gray and Kenny Kennard, trying not to be conspicuous. But as he approached the door leading beneath the stands to the locker room, two kids leaned over the railing above, their arms outstretched.

"Earl! Earl!" they screamed.

He looked up and smiled. Then he trotted forward, jumped, reached high and grabbed their hands.

Someday maybe they'd return the favor.

BLASTING FAST 14

A HALF HOUR BEFORE KICKOFF, O. J. Simpson and Earl Campbell met at midfield, shook hands and visited a couple of minutes while the San Francisco Forty-Niners and the Houston Oilers were warming up in the Astrodome. It was a casual but touching scene—the great old pro meeting the brilliant new one.

For O. J., this was the third game of his tenth season in a spectacular career which had seen him race for as many as 2,003 yards in a fourteen-game schedule. Now he was struggling to start again with a weak team and a weak knee, one still needing rehabilitation after surgery in his last season at Buffalo.

For Earl it was the third game of his first season, and he'd already become only the third rookie in National Football League history to rush for more than 100 yards in his first two games. With the newly-expanded sixteen-game schedule and his entire career ahead of him, he clearly was a threat to someday break Simpson's single-season record and Jim Brown's career mark of 12,312 yards in nine seasons for Cleveland.

Great running backs empathize with each other. Regardless of age or affiliation, they admire and appreciate each other, respecting their membership in an exclusive fraternity. O. J. had his problems now, but he smiled when he saw the guy he had last greeted in a tuxedo at the Heisman Trophy dinner.

"I just congratulated Earl on how things have been going for him," Simpson said later. "I told him I like his style, the way he does things. He's a humble guy. You'll see that, I think, in the real great runners like Walter Payton. They know they're good. They don't have to tell anybody.

"I just told him to stay healthy. The game's been good to me. It's obvious it's going to be good to him."

Earl's first two Oiler seasons fulfilled the Juice's forecast. He led the NFL in rushing both years. In 1978 he gained 1,450 yards on 302 carries, scoring thirteen touchdowns. In 1979 he had 1,697 on 368, scoring nineteen touchdowns. Those 3,147 yards on 670 carries gave him a thumping 4.7-yard average. Earl, indeed, was off and running, and the Oilers raced along with him.

In that early game against the Forty-Niners, Earl busted loose for gains of sixteen and eleven yards, as the Oilers drove for Toni Fritsch's late field goal and won, 20–19.

"Earl showed me he's tough," Simpson said afterward. "This was the first time I had seen him in a football uniform. I didn't realize he was built so low to the ground. He's a tough guy for a tackler to get any leverage on. The first guy to hit him may try to block him down and think he's through, but he runs so low that the next thing you know he's ten yards downfield.

"He runs like a halfback with that low build and a good, positive attitude when he carries the ball. He's looking, but he's kinda determined. He knows where he wants to get. He's just a class runner. His attitude toward the game is going to be an advantage to him because he's class all the way."

People throughout football will raise a glass to that.

When his own halfback, Billy Sims, won the Heisman the year after Earl did, Oklahoma coach Barry Switzer was proud but remained realistic. "Earl Campbell is the greatest player who ever suited up," he said. "Billy Sims is human. Campbell isn't."

University of Houston Coach Bill Yeoman expressed it as effectively but with a little more elegance. "Earl is a perfect example of increased productivity that this country needs. He's just worried about today and he's concerned about how he produces. It's like comparing a priest and the Pope when you talk about other runners and Earl."

During Earl's sensational senior year at Texas, Arkansas's Frank Broyles declared, "He is the most phenomenal player I've ever seen. He has the mobility of a 180-pounder. Now you put 220 pounds with that and you have something no one has ever seen. Jim Brown is the only player I would compare with Campbell."

Much traveled Sid Gillman, with pro football coaching experience spanning three decades, said simply, "Earl Campbell is the greatest football player I've ever seen."

San Diego Chargers coach Don Coryell tended to agree. "I don't know how anybody could be physically or mentally tougher. Earl has tremendous strength and balance, yet he has speed to run away from you. I don't know what more you could want. And he's a fierce competitor."

Ronnie Lee, who was Earl's teammate on the Texas state championship team at John Tyler High School in 1973 and later played tight end for Baylor University and the Miami Dolphins, noted, "At each level he's advanced—and makes it look easy. I guess you could say that Earl is just a person who was born to be great."

Calvin Hill, like O. J., began his career as a pro running back in 1969. He was an instant sensation with the Dallas Cowboys, a rangy, long-striding runner who, like Earl nine years later, earned All-Pro as well as Rookie of the Year honors. He left the Cowboys in 1975 for a year with Hawaii in the World Football League, then returned to the NFL for two years at Washington before finishing out the '70s with Cleveland. Like O. J., Hill has a great frame of reference when he talks about running backs.

And, like O. J., he has great respect for Campbell.

"Earl has the ideal build for a runner," says Hill, a man
of six feet, four-and-a-half inches and 230 pounds admiring
one of five-eleven and 224. "I watched him against Dallas
(Thanksgiving Day '79), and noticed how low to the ground
he runs. People talk about the punishment he takes, but
he deals it out. He never gets hit that much. He's agile
and he's strong. He's built like a bulldozer, but he's moving.

"He's in a class by himself."

"Earl may not be in a class by himself," says Bum Phillips, "but whatever class he's in, it sure doesn't take long
to call roll."

The Campbell style: swerving, slanting, crouching, blasting, exploding. He's blessed with the rare ability to get
low, keeping his balance and full control of his body. When
he's waiting for his blocking to develop and looking for
a crack in the defense, he moves with a leaning, sometimes
lurching, gait.

Mike Campbell, Texas's defensive coach during Earl's
first three years as a Longhorn, once said it reminded him
"of the way Groucho Marx looked when he walked."

But when he takes off, he really takes off. "Earl runs,"
said quarterback Dan Pastorini, "like he's got a rocket tied
to his tail and a gyroscope in his stomach."

Earl never wastes energy returning to the huddle after
he has been tackled. Like Jim Brown, he almost drags himself back. One might suspect Earl of dogging it—until he
tears into the next play.

"He gets up awful slow," said Phillips, "but he goes
down awful slow, too."

And there can be some fine moves in between.

"Earl jukes as many as he runs over," Simpson notes.
"He's a true halfback, and Jim Brown was a fullback."

So was Earl for three college seasons, being converted
to the Wishbone formation and slamming away at the inte-
rior defense after playing halfback in high school. When
Fred Akers succeeded Darrell Royal as Texas's head coach
and installed the Veer and I formations Earl continued

in a heavy-duty role, but he moved in more directions.

"We designed that offense around him," Akers says. "Earl's the kind of back you can call on to do a lot of different things. It took Earl a while to adjust from being a fullback. He could still do the inside running, but the outside game was a little different for him. He needed to learn to adjust his speed, to control it so blocking patterns could develop.

"He didn't fully develop that while he was with us. He came along real well with it his first two years with the Oilers but he still has had room for improvement."

Which is fine with Earl, who never has shown any sign of being satisfied with his talent as it is. He's a worker, and he appreciates all those who work with him, although those linemen he holds so dear sometimes have talked like they don't do much.

"Earl doesn't need a hole," Texas guard Jim Yarbrough once said, "just a crease. If you get just a piece of your man and hold him up for a second, Earl's gone. Nobody can arm-tackle him."

"Earl's the perfect back to block for," noted Rick Ingraham, another veteran Longhorn. "If I don't block my man perfectly, he'll run over him—sometimes him and me."

At Houston, as Earl began to hesitate and wait for plays to develop, he was an immediate delight.

"Blocking for Earl is a lot of fun," said tackle Greg Sampson after that remarkable rookie performance against Miami (199 yards, four touchdowns). "You know that if you get a fix on your man, there's a chance Earl will break it for a touchdown. In addition, he's very complimentary. He thanks us if we open a hole. And he keeps quiet if we haven't."

When Sampson fell seriously ill and required brain surgery during training camp the next summer, he was forced to retire. Determined to find a high-caliber replacement, Phillips gave the New England Patriots a No. 1 draft choice in a trade for all-pro Leon Gray.

Although he joined the team little more than a week before the regular-season opener at Washington, Gray

found he could learn the basics of his new offense with
no great difficulty.

"Bum told me to use straight-ahead blocking and wait
for Earl to come by."

Pete Wysocki, the Redskins' linebacker said it:

"Tackling Earl Campbell lowers your IQ."

Jack Tatum might not agree, but in his final Oakland
season before being traded to Houston, he did learn that
it can lower one's self-esteem.

The notorious free safety, whose savage pass coverage
had terrorized Lynn Swann and paralyzed Darryl Stingley,
found it was different bumping into a runner like Campbell.
But Tatum did a lot more than just bump. He blasted
him with all his fury when they met head-on at the Oakland
1-yard line at the Astrodome in November of 1979.

"I hit Campbell with my best shot," Tatum says. "I
bounced one way and he bounced the other. Somehow
he kept his feet, found his sense of direction, and scored.
I couldn't believe it."

"I just kept moving," says Earl.

He also has made a stunning impression on a lot of
would-be tacklers with his stiff-arm. He has dropped the
best defensive backs in pro football with it, leaving them
looking like they had stepped in an open manhole while
pursuing him. It can be a numbing experience. But Earl's
stiff arm is nothing new. C. C. Baker, the principal of John
Tyler High School, recalls talking with the athletic director
of Plano High School a few days after Tyler's playoff victory
over Plano during Earl's senior year.

"He told me they were puzzled how a little defensive
back got a concussion against us," Baker said, "and then
they saw it in the game film. It was an Earl Campbell! stiff-
arm."

After his 166-yard, two-touchdown performance enabled
the Oilers to catch Washington near the finish and win,
29–27, on a steaming Labor Day Sunday at RFK Stadium,
salutes to Earl were universal in the Redskin locker room.

"He showed a lot of guts," said Diron Talbert, the graybeard defensive tackle. "He took some good shots and he gave some good shots. He's so damn big.

"He's probably in the same class as Jim Brown and O. J. The thing is, he can run outside and inside."

"I usually don't watch the other offense when I'm on the sideline," said quarterback Joe Theismann, "but I did today. I wanted to see a great football player."

Isiah Robertson was an All-Pro linebacker for the Los Angeles Rams when he opposed Earl as a rookie. He couldn't stop him, or stop talking about him.

"Campbell is the toughest running back to bring down I've ever played against," Robertson declared. "The more you hit him, the faster, tougher, and stronger he gets. In this league, we're used to seeing moves. He gives you moves to get you off balance and then runs over you!"

Later television commentator Merlin Olsen referred to a replay of one such instance. "Isiah asked me not to show it," Olsen said. "He said the Rams were already calling him Grauman's Chinese Theater because of the footprints all over him."

Oiler offensive backfield coach Andy Bourgeois muses that it must be a terrible feeling in a defensive secondary when Earl breaks through the line.

"It reminds me of those malt liquor commercials where the bull bursts through the wall into a room," he says. "If those backs were having a party, Earl would sure break it up."

All of this awe doesn't surprise Darrell Royal.

"When I watched Earl in high school I saw the same thing we've seen right on through his career," says the retired University of Texas coach. "He was running over people, especially in the secondary. Everybody said, 'Well, he won't be able to do that when he gets with the big boys in college.' So he did it. Then they said, 'When he gets in the NFL he won't be doing that.' Well, he's still running over them.

"He is a truly great runner and he's powerful. I've never seen the first guy take him down in the secondary. Not if he's up and running. He has a tremendous stiff-arm, the most effective I've ever seen. His hand is huge. When he puts that big meat on somebody, that guy doesn't come any closer.

"Earl's balance is unbelievable. It was just breathtaking to see it when you just knew he was going to the ground. Some way or another he hits on his hand or suddenly seems to sprout a third leg, but he comes up with balance."

Campbell, for all his assets, also is blessed with a lower center of gravity than most people.

"You've seen these sports cars that squat like this when they take off?" asks Royal, tilting his hand at a forty-five-degree angle to demonstrate. "That's what Earl does. When those average backs take off they go up and down. But Earl just naturally sinks as he takes off. His old rear end just kind of ducks down and he's got that low gravity, you betcha, and tremendous thighs."

Those bulging thighs give Earl strength and explosiveness to get through heavy resistance. But fortunately he doesn't have a bulging head. His attitude about running with the football may be almost as valuable to him as his speed and his stiff-arm.

"He keeps everything in good perspective," Royal notes. "If he has a good day he doesn't get too high and if he has a bad day he doesn't get too low. He knows to just keep plugging and a good day will come. He's going to have more good ones than bad ones, and he's going to have some great ones. And then he's sometimes going to have a Pittsburgh game (the 1979 AFC championship battle). But I'll bet he handled that well, too. That wasn't necessarily Earl's fault, because all running backs look the same when they have no place to run."

Earl didn't show any great depression after that 27–13 loss to the Steelers killed the Oilers' Super Bowl hopes again. After missing a game and half of the playoffs with a pulled groin, he went to Pittsburgh fit and eager but never got untracked. The Steeler defenders jammed his running lanes and got the jump on the Oiler blockers by shooting gaps in the line, gambling they could stop Earl before he could escape for big gains. He averaged less than one yard per carry, netting just fifteen yards on seventeen tries, as a national television audience and a delighted crowd in Three Rivers Stadium saw the Steelers win.

Like anyone, Earl has bad games, and he absorbs punishment during the long season. He missed one full game and parts of others each of his first two Oiler seasons because of injuries. Some say he should not run so recklessly, that he should protect himself more. And they're always wondering how long he can last.

Earl and his coach feel he'll be around quite a while.

"I don't think I take any more punishment than anybody else," Earl said. "The name of the game is hit or be hit. I just go out and play, and let everybody else worry about that."

The fact that Earl carries the football with a bruising style befitting the linebacker he once was encouraged Bum Phillips to predict long life for him as a pro star.

"I think Earl will last forever," Bum said before his second season. "The guys who get hurt are the ones who are dodging people and suddenly get the hell knocked out of 'em. Earl's the punish-er, not the punish-ee. He's the hunt-er, not the hunt-ee.

"Sure, people remember how we lost him early in our second game with the Steelers when he was a rookie, but that was a freak injury. Just as the back hit him, Earl rolled and hit the turf—bam! The tackler didn't hurt him; slamming flat on that turf is what broke his rib."

Playing on artificial turf so often also takes its toll. Jim Brown, six-foot-two and 230, was a tremendous physical specimen who never missed a game during his nine years in the NFL. He also played his entire career on natural grass. In retrospect, that was a plus.

Seven games into his splendid senior season at Texas, Earl noted, "When I go to have coffee on Sunday morning I know how I'm doing by how sore my feet are from the artificial turf. If my feet aren't sore, I'll be in pretty good spirits. I haven't fallen on grass in so long I don't know what it would feel like."

Such aches are a part of the game Brown never knew.

But if Earl holds up to them and the rest of the punishment he should have a good shot at surpassing Brown's career yardage of 12,312.

While he doesn't have a lot of grass going for him, he does have a lot of games—sixteen per season. The NFL played a twelve-game schedule Brown's first four years, 1957–60, and increased it to fourteen his last five.

Men who have watched both Brown and Campbell closely made some interesting comparisons when Dale Robertson of the *Houston Post* talked to them.

"Jim didn't come into the league with the kind of build-up Earl had," said Dallas Cowboys scout John Wooten, a guard on the Cleveland teams of the Jim Brown era. "But, in terms of what they did to turn a franchise around, they're very similar. They both joined teams that were good enough already for them to make an immediate difference.

"Comparing Jim and Earl is more realistic than comparing Jim with O. J. or Earl with O. J. Their running styles are more alike, and they both have the great natural strength that's so obvious when they run. Earl is closer to being like Jim than anybody I've seen come into the league since then."

Former Cowboy assistant coach Ray Renfro, a wide receiver at Cleveland and father of Oiler wide receiver Mike Renfro, thought Earl has a greater impact than the larger Brown.

"Jim was more of an upright runner, and he didn't punish tacklers like Earl does," Ray says. "He's the most punishing runner I've ever seen. Jim seldom ran over defensive backs if he didn't have to, but Earl runs over anybody who gets in his way—backs, linebackers, or linemen. Jim had sprinter's speed, but he didn't have Earl's power.

"At the same time, a lot of people don't realize how quick Earl is. I saw it in him when he was still in high school, when his Tyler team played Mike's Arlington Heights team in the state playoffs. Mike was at cornerback on one play when Earl got loose up the middle. Mike hesitated a moment and lost his angle on him. Earl was gone.

No one caught him. I thought then he had the potential to be one of the best."

As personalities, the two great runners are entirely different. Brown was aloof, with no interest in being a team player or blocking.

"Jim had a complex that must have started as a kid," Renfro said. "I don't remember him having many close friends on the team. I never really understood him. As far as comparing Earl and Jim as people, there is no comparison. Gosh, I doubt anybody could handle success better than Earl. People are going to remember him for the kind of person he was ten years after he's finished playing football."

In some ways, Earl never is out of season.

THE GREATEST REWARDS

E<small>ARL</small> C<small>AMPBELL</small> <small>LIVES</small> <small>CALMLY</small> and confidently, not because he's certain each day will be a great one but because he knows there is a good reason for it being what it is.

"The Lord is in control of my life," he has said. "Whatever I'm able to do is up to him. All I can do is work and pray and give whatever I do my best effort. After I'm satisfied I've done that, then I know the rest is up to him.

"He's not going to make it easy. In fact, you show me a successful man—successful by whatever measure you want to choose—and I'll show you a man who has had his share of bumps and bruises and failures along the way. That's the way life works."

Like his life, Earl's extraordinary football career has not been without hurt and disappointment. As a high school junior he suddenly went from standout to outcast when his coach suspended him and four teammates for cutting classes the day of the final game. His junior season at the University of Texas was a major disappointment because leg injuries hindered him most of the time and forced him to the sideline for almost half the year. And his second

169

season with the Houston Oilers finished dismally in that
27–13 loss to Pittsburgh.

It was disappointing to end the season in failure, but
a classic example of Earl's own theory that any successful
man will know pain and failure in life. Before the Pittsburgh
game he had missed the last six quarters of playoff games
with San Diego and Denver because of a groin strain, but
he had refused to use the injury as an alibi.

"I was confident," he said, "but I guess they were more
confident. They just put a lot of guys on the line of scrimmage and did a great job."

At times like these Earl speaks softly and evenly, the
same as he does after fine performances. After all, this is
part of the same life. He likes to recall the words from a
Lou Rawls song: "The sun's gonna come up tomorrow."

"It won't get Earl down," his mother has said after a
game goes wrong. "He's lost before and he's won before
and I can guarantee you one thing: He's gonna win again."

Ann Campbell taught her children to appreciate the
good side of any situation. Thus Earl can truly enjoy
the caring of the fans who cheer his team in defeat, like the
Sunday night seventy thousand people jammed into the
Astrodome to welcome the Oilers home after Pittsburgh
had slammed the door to the Super Bowl again. And he
sincerely rejoices in the success of teammates when he
can't help them.

He showed this after the 1979 playoff game with San
Diego. The trip to San Diego seemed futile for the Oilers
because Earl and quarterback Dan Pastorini were sidelined.
The explosive Chargers were strong favorites to win and
then challenge Pittsburgh for the conference championship. Instead, the Oilers pulled a 17–14 upset, with outstanding performances by Vernon Perry, Rob Carpenter,
Gifford Nielsen, and Mike Renfro. It was an afternoon
which brought some new heroes to the front, and an exhila-
rating esprit de corps filled the locker room. No one felt
prouder than Earl, who realizes that sometimes there's a
reward in watching others do it.

"A lot of people have said this is a one-man team," he

said, "but now they've seen it's not. They saw a lot of players put it on the line when they had to. I tell you, I'm really proud of this bunch."

During his triumphant trip to New York for the Heisman Trophy dinner as a college senior, Earl expressed feelings about life which have held up well through the years: "My philosophy is being a man as well as a football player," he said. "I am not a machine. I'm just an easy-going country boy who likes to meet a lot of good people."

And good people, in Earl's mind, are where you find them.

"I can get along with people," he declares. "I have always respected those I have played against. I am not a black man. I am a man. I don't know anything about colors."

Although Earl likes to meet a lot of different people, he has never been a ladies' man. There has always been just one woman in his life—Reuna, his girlfriend from the ninth grade who has calmed him and gotten him going over the years. After he won the Heisman, he made it clear that all the attention he received from the fairer sex wherever he went meant nothing to him. There was only Reuna, who at that time was attending Tyler Junior College.

"She loved me when I had one pair of torn jeans," he said. "These other ladies like me because I'm Number 20. I'd rather have someone who loves me for what I am, just Earl."

He still feels that way. In May of 1980 Earl and Reuna married, convinced that they are as right for each other now as they had been at Moore Junior High.

Earl Campbell is a man who wears well. Over and over his friends, his coaches, his teammates describe him as warm and genuine, unspoiled by his phenomenal success.

"I've never been associated with a young man more sincere than Earl is," Fred Akers once said. "He genuinely cares about people—about you, about me, his family, teammates, other students on the campus.

"His football ability is just one of the things that impresses me about him. I believe his sincerity and dedication and his religious convictions will bring him his greatest success."

Akers's assessment of Earl as a total person remains valid. He does care about others, and he shows it.

When the Professional Football Writers of America again voted Earl the Most Valuable Player in the National Football League, he went to New York to accept the award, and took tough-blocking fullback Tim Wilson with him.

"I had a lot of people working for me," he said. "That's why I brought Tim Wilson along. It's my way of saying, 'Thank you, Tim,' and saying thank you to the rest of the team."

Lynn King, another fullback who threw a lot of key blocks for Earl in high school, always has appreciated the consistency in the Campbell personality.

"Earl is a leader in his own easygoing way," King says. "Nothing ever affected him. He's the same now as he was then. Everything they say about him is true. I know, because I knew him then."

Darrell Royal also thinks of him as much more than a football star. "Earl has more common sense than a lot of Ph.D.s," he says, "He just has a gut feel for the right thing to say, and how to handle situations."

Their relationship, always good, has grown closer since Royal retired from coaching.

"Earl is a warm person and he likes to visit," Royal says. "He'd come by the house and he might lie down on the floor. I remember one time he was draped over a little bitty piano bench. You can imagine how much of him was hanging off, but he must have stayed on that bench for an hour. He just curled up as much as he could, turned over occasionally and talked about whatever came along."

His religious beliefs wear as well as he does. He's not a preacher or a teacher, nor does he want to be considered a flawless example of Christian living, but he does express himself sincerely.

"I believe in God and he helps me," Earl says. "If things

are going good, I say, 'Thank you.' If they're going bad, I say, 'Don't remove all my stumbling blocks. Just give me strength.'

"I don't want to be thought of as someone who does the right thing all the time, and people shouldn't pattern themselves after me. I believe in God, and my faith is not a part-time thing. I try to do my best, but if my best is wrong, that will have to be it."

In all the years since he outgrew his life as Bad Earl, however, his best has been right with his mother.

"Since Earl put his bad time behind him," Ann Campbell says, "I've been tremendously proud of him, just the way I feel about all my children. I feel the same love and concern for all of them.

"The way he has handled his success has been valuable to the whole family. When he was in college and a big star and came home, he just came in that old house and got in bed and slept with his brothers, just like he always had. He's always just been one of the children.

"If he had handled it differently, they might have handled it differently. But there's never been any problem. It's just been beautiful."

The same warm feeling exists in the new house Earl built for his mother. When he came home for a weekend and the word got around, the house was packed with friends. This delayed visiting with his family, but the Campbells are stayers.

"He was up with his brothers and sisters at three-thirty in the morning," Ann says, "sitting around the fireplace, talking and laughing, and having a great time. It was just like it's always been."

And her life in that lovely home on Farm Road 492 has changed in some ways but not in others.

"I don't go a lot of places that I could, accept invitations for trips and other occasions," she said. "I've reached a time in my life when I can set my own pace and do what I want to do."

Obviously, what she wants to do is be with her family, go to church, and enjoy her friends. Her children, as always, know they can count on Mama for anything. When I was visiting her once she went to the phone for a few minutes. Steve, who was living in Austin, had called and asked her how to make brown gravy.

"That's nothing," she said, laughing. "One time Martha called me from Germany and asked, 'Mama, how do you stuff a turkey?' "

Ann Campbell exudes good feeling, fairness and friendship. No one is a stranger to her for long.

After she returned from the Heisman Trophy dinner in New York, she received a long distance call from Barbara Washington, a young schoolteacher in St. Louis.

"I saw you on television," she told Ann. "I admire you and I want to be your friend. I'd like to come and visit you."

"That would be nice, Barbara," Ann said, "but I want you to know we don't live real fancy."

"Mrs. Campbell, I cut tobacco in South Carolina," Barbara replied. "I know what it's all about."

Barbara came to visit and they became good friends. After the new house was built, Barbara visited again and brought her two-year-old child. When Ann was driving them to the airport, Barbara told her how much she appreciated her kindness and hospitality.

"Barbara," Ann told her softly, "you're just thirsty for a family."

Finding a new friend by long distance pleased Ann, but it didn't surprise her.

"You don't have to live near," she said, "to be neighbors."

Although her children, grandchildren and other relatives grow very excited about watching Earl's games on the giant screen TV in the family room, Ann doesn't allow football to interfere with church. If the game starts at noon on Sunday, it may be almost halftime before she turns it on. And if there is a later kickoff, she may get in her car and head back to Hopewell Baptist No. 1 without seeing the finish.

"We have several choirs and do quite a bit of singing,"

she said. "If we have a program at two-thirty or three, well, I don't let football hold me up. I watch it while I'm home, but when it comes time to go I just go. I'll hear about the rest of it later."

Ann Campbell clearly has been a tremendous influence on Earl and her ten other children. She is a woman of unusual strength and confidence, who not only provided for them but guided and inspired them. Her deep faith in God sustained her through a lot of hard years, but her personal drive cannot be underestimated.

"I remember seeing Hugh Downs interview her on "20/20," when they had a feature on Earl," Darrell Royal says. "He asked her, 'Why do you think it is that you with no husband and all those children were able to be as successful in rearing them as you have been, when so many others have failed?'

"She paused just ever so slightly, then said, 'Maybe they didn't try.' She had that little glint in her eye, and that smile, and they left that expression on the screen in a freeze-frame. That said a lot."

Earl Campbell became a hero instead of a tragedy because he felt the driving force in his life. There was the driving force of God, of course. And there was the driving force of a woman with too much love and faith to ever give up. So the confused kid who ran that blacktop road kept going, and growing. It's enough to make a mama proud, all right.